INTERMEDIATE 2

INFORMATION SYSTEMS
2007-2011

2007 EXAM — page 3
2008 EXAM — page 17
2009 EXAM — page 33
2010 EXAM — page 51
2011 EXAM — page 73
ANSWER SECTION — page 97

Publisher's Note

We are delighted to bring you the 2011 Past Papers and you will see that we have changed the format from previous editions. As part of our environmental awareness strategy, we have attempted to make these new editions as sustainable as possible.
To do this, we have printed on white paper and bound the answer sections into the book. This not only allows us to use significantly less paper but we are also, for the first time, able to source all the materials from sustainable sources.

We hope you like the new editions and by purchasing this product, you are not only supporting an independent Scottish publishing company but you are also, in the International Year of Forests, not contributing to the destruction of the world's forests.

Thank you for your support and please see the following websites for more information to support the above statement –

www.fsc-uk.org

www.loveforests.com

© Scottish Qualifications Authority
All rights reserved. Copying prohibited. No part of this publication may be reproduced, stored in a retrieval system, or transmitted in any form or by any means, electronic, mechanical, photocopying, recording or otherwise.

First exam published in 2007.
Published by Bright Red Publishing Ltd, 6 Stafford Street, Edinburgh EH3 7AU
tel: 0131 220 5804 fax: 0131 220 6710 info@brightredpublishing.co.uk www.brightredpublishing.co.uk

ISBN 978-1-84948-201-1

A CIP Catalogue record for this book is available from the British Library.

Bright Red Publishing is grateful to the copyright holders, as credited on the final page of the Question Section, for permission to use their material. Every effort has been made to trace the copyright holders and to obtain their permission for the use of copyright material. Bright Red Publishing will be happy to receive information allowing us to rectify any error or omission in future editions.

INTERMEDIATE 2
2007

X216/201

NATIONAL
QUALIFICATIONS
2007

THURSDAY, 24 MAY
9.00 AM – 10.30 AM

INFORMATION
SYSTEMS
INTERMEDIATE 2

Attempt Sections 1 and 2 and **one part** of Section 3.

Sections 1 and 2 — Attempt all questions within these sections.

Section 3 — This section has three parts:

    Part A—Applied Multimedia

    Part B—Expert Systems

    Part C—The Internet

Choose **one** part of this section and attempt all of the questions within that part.

Read all questions carefully.

Write your answers in the answer book provided. Do not write on the question paper.

Write as neatly as possible.

SECTION 1

Attempt all questions in this section.

1. What is an entity in a relational database?

2. A database has a field of type *link*.

   Give an example of what might be found in this type of field.

3. A car showroom keeps information about vehicles it has to sell in a database. Part of the database has been sorted as shown below.

Make	Model	Year of Registration	Mileage
Renoir	Chloe	2001	37564
Pursio	205	2001	36542
Jokeswagon	Tennis	2001	35004
Renoir	Magritte	2002	45089
Renoir	Chloe	2002	24659
Missan	Nicra	2004	15487

   Describe how the list has been sorted.

4. An employee is entering data into a database but misses out one of the fields. As a consequence this message appears on the screen: "The field called 'reference number' cannot be left empty. A value must be typed into this field".

   Explain why this message appeared.

5. A company rents out cottages to holidaymakers. The list of cottages is updated regularly. For each booking the total cost is calculated and is printed in alphabetical order.

Name	Location	Rental Price	Weeks booked	Total Cost
Forrest View	Woodtown	£350	1	£350
Seaview Cottage	Brightpool	£450	2	£900
Shore Cottage	Blackon	£400	2	£800
TreeTops	Woodtown	£300	3	£900

   You are asked to create the list using either word processing or spreadsheet software.

   Which application type is more suitable for this job?

   Justify your choice.

Marks

6. State **one** action an employer could take to reduce the risk of repetitive strain injury (RSI) for employees. 1

7. (a) What is meant by *information intellectual property rights*? 1

(b) Why is it important to safeguard such rights? 1

8. A hacker illegally accesses a bank computer system and transfers money out of some accounts. Which Act does this breach? 1

9. A travel agency closes its High Street shops and sells its holidays via its website.

(a) State **one** economic implication of this for the company. 1

(b) State **one** economic implication for employees. 1

10. Shoppers are asked to register on a website before purchasing goods. Here is part of the data input form used to gather information about each shopper.

Forename _____ Surname _____

Tick box if you wish to be added to our mailing list ☐

Date of Birth ☐☐ / ☐☐ / ☐☐

Suggest the most suitable data type for the following fields.

(a) Mailing list 1

(b) Date of Birth 1

Total for Section 1 (15)

[END OF SECTION 1]

[Turn over

SECTION 2

Attempt all questions in this section.

11. The *efficiency* of an Information System is determined by the *speed*, *accuracy* and *volume* of the data that is processed.

    (a) What is meant by "volume" of information? — 1

    (b) Describe the role of a *knowledge worker*. — 2

    (c) State **one** example of a "knowledge worker". — 1

    (4)

12. An estate agency buys and sells property. It has a website to advertise the properties and networked computers in its main office to manage its information system. The network is connected to a centralised database.

    (a) What type of applications software should be used to

        (i) create the website? — 1

        (ii) view the website? — 1

    (b) The estate agency has put in place a *network strategy* and a *security strategy*.

        (i) State **two** reasons why the estate agency needs to have a "security strategy". — 2

        (ii) State **two** other strategies that the estate agency would be advised to put in place. — 2

    (c) The data is held on one central computer. State **three** advantages of having a centralised database. — 3

    (9)

13. (a) Explain **two** benefits of an electronic database compared with a manual database. — 2

    (b) Explain what is meant by the term *data modelling*. — 2

    (c) What is meant by a single valued field? — 1

    It is very common to find duplication of data in a flat file database. This can lead to data becoming inconsistent.

    (d) (i) What type of database should be used to reduce duplication of data and inconsistency? — 1

        (ii) State **one** way in which it reduces duplication. — 1

    (7)

14. The table below shows an extract from a flat file database about sports.

Instructor and Class

Instructor ID	Instructor Name	ClassCode	SportClass	Level	CostPerclass
JS72	John Smith	JAV1	Javelin	1	£32
		SP1	Sprint	1	£32
		HD1	Hurdles	1	£34
MH82	Mary Hughes	LJ1	Long Jump	1	£28
		SP2	Sprint	2	£25
		TJ1	Triple Jump	1	£25
JG92	John Grant	HD2	Hurdles	2	£38
		JAV2	Javelin	2	£38
		HJ1	High Jump	1	£38

(a) (i) Normalise the above table by removing the multi-valued fields, and show how it would be represented in two tables. Identify the Primary keys and Foreign key in the new tables. **7**

(ii) State the purpose of a *key* in a table. **1**

(b) State what the relationship is between the tables. **2**

(10)

Total for Section 2 **(30)**

[END OF SECTION 2]

[Turn over

SECTION 3

PART A—Applied Multimedia

Marks

15. A local museum plans to provide an electronic public information point. It will provide information about the museum and its displays.

(a) (i) Recommend an appropriate delivery medium for the museum to use in this situation. **1**

(ii) State **two** reasons why this could be the preferred choice of delivery by the museum. **2**

(b) What input device would be most suitable for members of the public to use to access the information about the museum? **1**

(c) The company constructing the multimedia application have to take account of more than the delivery media.

State **two** other aspects that make up the analysis stage of development and state a reason for the inclusion of **each** aspect. **4**

(d) The application includes audio files. Describe **two** methods by which the size of the files could be reduced. **2**

(10)

16. A business multimedia application allows users to navigate from any screen directly to any other screen.

(a) Which type of navigation structure would be most appropriate for this application? **1**

Part of the application allows users to enter their personal details to be sent further information about products.

(b) Which piece of legislation protects users' details submitted in this way? **1**

(c) (i) Which type of user interface should the designer use to allow submission of users' details? **1**

(ii) Give a reason for your answer. **1**

(d) State **two** techniques that can be used to navigate through a multimedia application. **2**

(e) The text in the application included a number of *lists*. State **two** other means by which text may be clearly displayed. **2**

(8)

Marks

17. A company is producing a multimedia application for children. They wish to include cartoon characters from popular TV shows.

(a) The graphic designer is worried about the inclusion of these characters.

Explain why she should be worried about including these characters. **1**

(b) Some illustrations will be cartoon drawings and others will be full colour photographs. All the illustrations will require editing and manipulating. The designer has graphics software that can create *bitmapped* or *vector* graphics.

Which type of graphics software should be used for

(i) the cartoon drawings? **1**

(ii) the full colour photographs? **1**

(c) The application includes over 1,500 photographs. The graphic designer has been instructed to reduce the overall storage requirements for these photographs. Describe **two** methods by which this could be done. **2**

(d) Once the application has been completed, extensive testing is carried out. Explain the purpose of:

(i) screen tests; **1**

(ii) navigation tests. **1**

(7)

Total for Section 3 Part A **(25)**

[*END OF SECTION 3—PART A*]

[Turn over

SECTION 3

PART B—Expert Systems

18. The diagram below shows how a user interacts with an expert system.

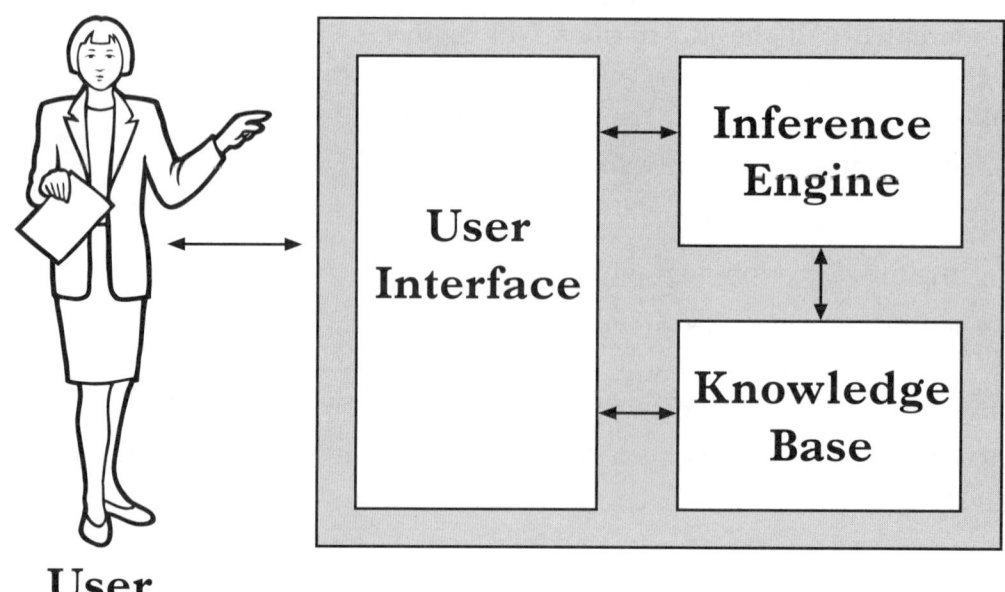

(a) State **one** purpose of an expert system. 1

(b) Describe the main features of the following components:

(i) Knowledge Base 1

(ii) Inference Engine 1

(c) The User Interface is used to display questions to the user and obtain answers. It is also used to display advice and justification.

Describe **two** features used to evaluate the quality of the user interface. 2

(d) Describe **two** justification facilities which would be available in an expert system. 2

(7)

19. A nature reserve currently provides information sheets to visitors to help them identify butterflies they can see around the nature reserve.

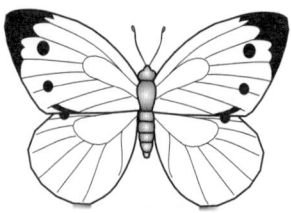

An expert system is being introduced into the visitor centre to replace the information sheets.

(a) What category of expert system would the nature reserve use to identify the butterflies? 1

Many people are involved in developing the expert system for the nature reserve.

(b) Explain the roles of the following personnel in this situation:

(i) domain expert 1

(ii) knowledge engineer 1

19. (continued)

(c) Part of the knowledge is represented in a decision tree.

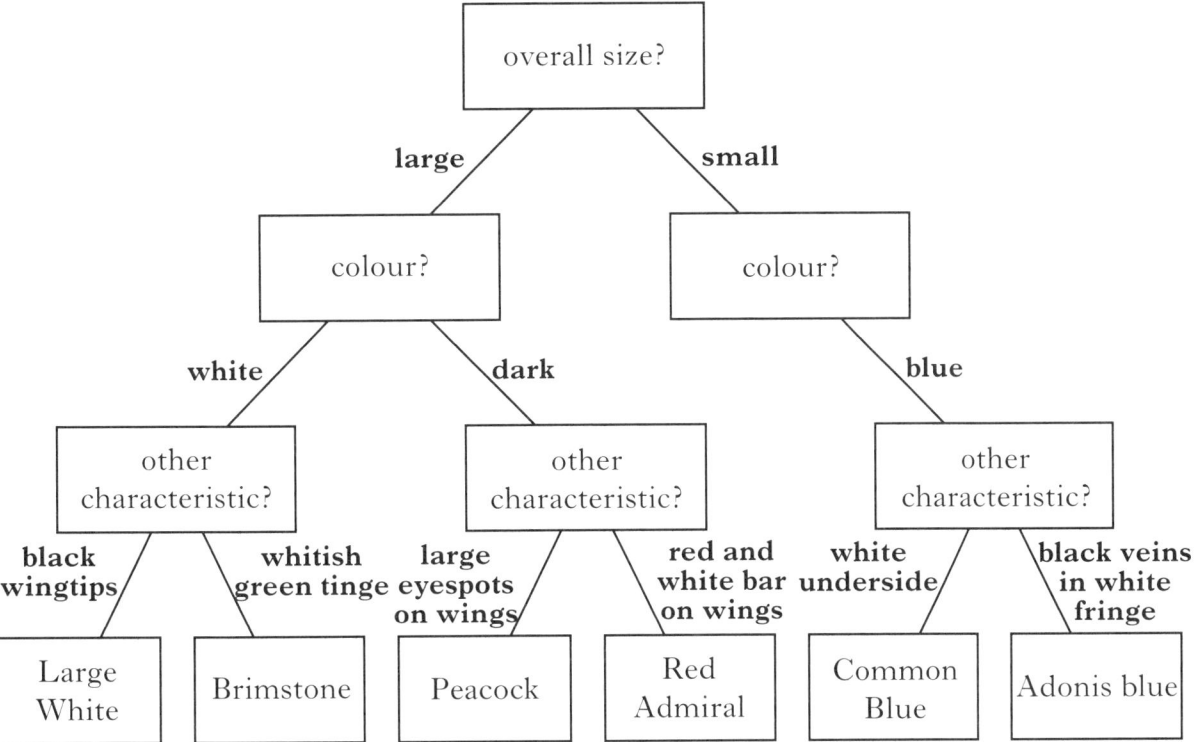

This is used to write the following production rule.
IF   overall size IS large
AND   colour IS white
AND   other characteristic IS black wingtips
THEN   butterfly type IS large white

(i) Design production rules for **two** other types of butterflies using the information in the decision tree. 4

(ii) Identify the method of *inferencing* that has been used in the rule above. 1

(d) The final stage of developing the expert system is *system validation*. Describe **one** technique used to carry out "system validation". 1

(9)

[Turn over

Marks

20. A printer manufacturer wants to develop an expert system to use on their helpdesk to determine the nature of problems with ink jet printers. Here is some of the knowledge to be included in the system.

> "Each printer has two lights—a red one and an amber one. If the red light is flashing and the amber light is off then the problem is the paper is jammed. When the red light is on and the amber light is off then the paper tray is completely empty and must be refilled. The amber light flashes to indicate the ink cartridge is low, while an empty ink cartridge is indicated by the amber light on. In both these cases, the red light is off. If both the red light and amber light are on, then the service engineer needs to be called to attend to the problem."

Represent the knowledge about the printer problems as a factor table.

(5)

21. Here is a table showing information about snowboards.

Shape	Flexibility	Size	Type of Snowboard
Directional	Soft	Narrow	Freerider
Directional Twin	Very Soft	Wide	Freestyle
Directional	Stiff	Very Narrow	Racing

The information could be put into an expert system or into a database.

(a) How many records would be in the database?

(b) How many rules would be in the expert system?

(c) How many fields would make up each record in the database?

(d) How many conditions would each rule have in the expert system?

(4)

Total for Section 3 Part B (25)

[END OF SECTION 3—PART B]

SECTION 3

PART C—The Internet

22. A family are planning a weekend break and wish to book a hotel room on-line. Their favourite hotel chain is called the Valiant Group which owns hundreds of hotels throughout the UK and abroad. Each hotel has different facilities.

(a) They use an Internet search engine to find a Valiant hotel with a swimming pool, anywhere except London. Write down a Boolean search that would produce the required results. **3**

(b) When they make their reservation with the hotel their details are stored in a database and they receive a booking reference number.

  (i) What piece of legislation protects information stored in this way? **1**

  (ii) Why is the booking reference number required? **1**

(c) They wish to download a file containing a map showing directions to the hotel. Which protocol will they use? **1**

(d) They notice that their browser is showing the *IP address* of the server containing the file. What is an "IP address"? **1**

(e) Communication takes place between the family and the hotel by e-mail.

  Name the protocols used for:

  (i) sending e-mails; **1**

  (ii) receiving e-mails. **1**

  (9)

23. A multinational company is holding a conference at one of the Valiant hotels.

(a) Some people attending the conference have laptop computers but all of the attendees need to access the Internet.

  Name **one** other portable device they might use to access the Internet. **1**

(b) The attendees communicate with each other using *newsgroups* and *chat*. Describe the difference in communication method between "newsgroups" and "chat". **2**

(c) On the second day of the conference, a group of attendees intends to participate in a *video conference* with company employees in Berlin.

  (i) What extra piece of hardware would the participants require? **1**

  (ii) State **one** advantage to the company and **one** advantage to the employees of using "video conferencing". **2**

  (6)

[Turn over for Question 24 on Page twelve

Marks

24. The Valiant group has a centralised booking system, and each hotel has its own website.

Helen Pertwee's job is to create, maintain and update each of the hotel websites.

(a) She uses web authoring software to create the web pages. The software has a *hyperlink tool*. What is the purpose of the "hyperlink tool"? **1**

(b) She has to decide whether the hyperlinks use *absolute page addressing* or *relative page addressing*.

   (i) Describe how "absolute page addressing" works. **1**

   (ii) Describe **two** advantages of "relative page addressing". **2**

(c) Helen finds that her page with a photograph on it takes a long time to load. What could Helen do to the photograph to make it load faster? **1**

(d) Each hotel has its own intranet with workstations, a *multiplexer* and a *router*. Through this, guests can access the Internet.

   (i) Describe the purpose of a "multiplexer". **1**

   (ii) Describe the function of the "router". **2**

(e) What must Helen do to keep the computers protected from *viruses*? **2**

(10)

Total for Section 3 Part C (25)

[END OF SECTION 3—PART C]

[END OF QUESTION PAPER]

INTERMEDIATE 2
2008

[BLANK PAGE]

X216/201

NATIONAL
QUALIFICATIONS
2008

MONDAY, 19 MAY
9.00 AM – 10.30 AM

INFORMATION SYSTEMS
INTERMEDIATE 2

Attempt Section I and Section II and **one** Part of Section III.

Section I – Attempt all questions.

Section II – Attempt all questions.

Section III – This section has three parts:

        Part A – Applied Multimedia
        Part B – Expert Systems
        Part C – The Internet

Choose **one** part and answer **all** of the questions in that part.

Read each question carefully.

Write your answers in the answer book provided. **Do not** write on the question paper.

Write as neatly as possible.

Answer in sentences wherever possible.

SECTION I

Attempt all questions in this section.

1. What type of application software would you recommend to allow users to communicate across the Internet in real-time?

2. Here is the design for a pupil database.

Field Name	Data Type	Sample Data
Forename	text	Lidia
Surname	text	Witkiewicz
Class	text	4B
Subjects	text	English, Computing, Gaelic, Art

   State the term used to describe text fields such as *Subjects*.

3. State **two** offences covered by the Computer Misuse Act 1990.

4. What is *on-line* help?

5. Name the object in a spreadsheet that contains a single piece of text, a number or a formula.

6. State **one** security method that may be used by an organisation to ensure a hacker cannot access data.

Marks

7.
> When travelling to a foreign country it is important to have a passport with you. A passport is a document that identifies you as a citizen of the country that issues the passport.
>
> At an airport or ferry port there is usually someone inspecting passports, and they will use an ink stamp to mark your passport, showing that you have entered a new country.

The diagram above shows a small part of a word processed document.

(a) Identify **one** data object from the text above.   1

(b) Name **one** operation that could be performed on this data object.   1

8. Data has to be gathered and stored before it can be processed.

   State **two** electronic methods that allow large amounts of data to be gathered.   2

9. State **two** advantages of purchasing music on-line.   2

10. Explain why typing an e-mail message in capitals is seen as poor *netiquette*.   1

11. A piece of computer software offers users menus and keyboard commands to perform various tasks. Explain why the software offers users these different types of HCI.   1

Total for Section I (15)

[*END OF SECTION I*]

[**Turn over**

SECTION II

Attempt all questions in this section.

12. (a) A database is a collection of related information about people or objects. Many databases use manual data storage.

    State **three** problems that are associated with manual databases. — 3

    (b) State **one** advantage of an electronic database over a manual system. — 1

    (c) Two types of computerised database are *flat file* and *relational*.

    (i) What is meant by a "flat file" database? — 1

    (ii) State **two** limitations of a "flat file" database. — 2

    (d) *Normalisation* is a process used when a relational database is being designed.

    State **three** reasons why "normalisation" is required when using a relational model. — 3

    (10)

13. The data cards below show part of the database used by a music teacher to keep track of pupils and the instruments they are given.

    | Pupil ID | 023 |
    | First Name | John |
    | Second Name | Murnie |

Reference No.	Musical Instrument	Make
G78	Guitar	Fenbar
D34	Drums	Gudwig

    | Pupil ID | 058 |
    | First Name | Shuna |
    | Second Name | Ali |

Reference No.	Musical Instrument	Make
C18	Clarinet	Boyd
R12	Recorder	Sprat

    (a) (i) Normalise the data shown above by removing the multi-value fields. Identify the Primary and Foreign keys. — 7

    (ii) State the relationship between the entities created in (a)(i). — 1

    (b) When the database is implemented, the content of the field *Musical Instrument* is limited to certain values.

    Name this validation check. — 1

    (c) When the database is implemented, suggest the most suitable field type for *Reference No.* — 1

    (10)

[X216/201] *Page four*

Marks

14. Apple Bay High School has a policy of healthy eating in the school. The school student council wants to publicise the policy.

   The student council are to produce a special healthy eating information brochure containing pictures, alongside recipes and nutritional advice.

   (a) (i) What type of application software would be most suitable for this purpose? **1**

   (ii) State **two** reasons for your answer. **2**

   (b) The student council wants to include a picture of the student who won the "best recipe" competition.

   What will they have to do before they are allowed to include the picture in the brochure? **1**

   (c) The school has a database of all the people who received a copy of the brochure. A local health club requests a copy of the database. Why should the school not supply the database to the health club? **1**

   (d) The student council wants to promote their healthy eating policy by creating a website.

   (i) What type of application software should be used to construct the website? **1**

   (ii) State **two** advantages to the student council of using a website instead of the brochure. **2**

   (e) Some of the families associated with Apple Bay High School are described as being *information poor*.

   (i) Explain what is meant by "information poor". **1**

   (ii) State **one** disadvantage that arises from this. **1**

   (10)

   Total for Section II **(30)**

[*END OF SECTION II*]

[*Turn over*

SECTION III

Attempt ONE part of Section III

Part A	Applied Multimedia	Page 7	Questions 15 to 16
Part B	Expert Systems	Page 9	Questions 17 to 19
Part C	The Internet	Page 11	Questions 20 to 22

Choose **one** part and answer **all** of the questions in that part.

SECTION III

PART A—Applied Multimedia

Attempt ALL questions in this section.

15. A low cost air travel company wishes to update its website. This new website will be the only method customers have to book flights.

    (a) Suggest **two** reasons why the company is using the website as the only method of booking flights. **2**

    (b) When booking a flight, the customer sees the following screen.

    (i) State the type of search facility shown above. **1**

    (ii) State the type of user interface being used above. **1**

    (iii) State **one** reason why this type of interface has been chosen. **1**

    (c) Once the flights have been chosen, the customer will need to supply their personal details. Which type of user interface would you suggest for this Web page? **1**

    (d) State the job title of the specialist who creates the Web pages for customers to use. **1**

    (e) The company wishes to test the website before it is uploaded to the Internet. A group of customers is asked to test and evaluate the website.

    (i) Explain why the pages need to be tested. **1**

    (ii) State **one** method of testing the website they might use. **1**

    (iii) State the reason why the evaluation would be useful. **1**

    (10)

[Turn over

Marks

16. Eryn is an audio media specialist. She is working on a *CAL* storybook project. The project is a multimedia program that combines text and pictures with the audio of the stories being read.

(a) (i) What does "CAL" stand for? **1**

    (ii) Suggest **one** reason why an audio recording of the story would make this a better program. **1**

(b) There is limited storage capacity for Eryn's audio recordings.

    Describe **one** method of reducing the storage requirements for the audio recordings. **1**

(c) Laura is the project manager. She wishes audio to be added to the main screen.

StoryTelling Books
1. Black Beauty
2. A Christmas Carol
3. Little Women
4. Robin Hood
5. Treasure Island

    (i) State **two** possible uses of audio on this screen. **2**

    (ii) Draw the navigation map for this screen. **1**

    (iii) Name this type of navigation structure. **1**

    (iv) State which type of multimedia authoring software you would recommend to create this application. **1**

    (v) Give **one** reason for your choice. **1**

(d) Each book title has a *link* to a new screen. What is a "link"? **1**

(e) A *Transition* occurs when one screen changes to another.

    (i) What is a "transition"? **1**

    (ii) Explain why a "transition" might be used. **1**

(f) Once the program has been completed, various pieces of user documentation are written.

    (i) Describe the purpose of user instructions. **1**

    (ii) Explain why hardware and software system requirements are important when buying the program. **1**

(g) Which piece of legislation covers illegal copying of software? **1**

(15)

Total for Section III Part A (25)

[END OF SECTION III—PART A—APPLIED MULTIMEDIA]

Marks

SECTION III

PART B—Expert Systems

Attempt ALL questions in this section.

17. Dovaphone is a mobile phone company that offers several options to its customers who want a monthly contract. Dovaphone is considering implementing an expert system to help customers select the most suitable option for their needs.

    (a) State the category of the proposed expert system. **1**

    (b) The first stage of developing an expert system is called *knowledge acquisition*.

    State **two** methods used for "knowledge acquisition". **2**

    (c) Some of the knowledge acquired is represented as the following attribute-value pairs.

    Option 1 (minutes=100, text messages=50, WAP bundle=No)
    Option 2 (minutes=100, text messages=100, WAP bundle=No)
    Option 3 (minutes=100, text messages=100, WAP bundle=Yes)
    Option 4 (minutes=200, text messages=100, WAP bundle=No)
    Option 5 (minutes=200, text messages=100, WAP bundle=Yes)

    (i) Represent the attribute-value pairs as a decision tree. **5**

    (ii) Who would be responsible for creating this representation during the development of the expert system? **1**

    (9)

18. Dovaphone provides a range of mobile phones in their shops. The details about the features available on each model are currently held in a database. To help a customer select a suitable phone, the salesperson enters the customer's answers to a number of questions about their phone needs into the database system.

    The company decides to replace the database system with an expert system.

    (a) One advantage of an expert system is that it can provide *justification*.

    (i) State **two** types of "justification". **2**

    (ii) State **two** benefits to the customer of "justification" facilities in this expert system. **2**

    (b) Compare the output obtained from a database system and an expert system. **2**

    (c) Describe how the company would test the new expert system. **2**

    (8)

[Turn over

Marks

19. Motor racing cars can have 3 different types of tyres—Slicks, Intermediates or Wets—fitted during a race depending on the weather and track conditions.

An expert system is to be used to indicate the most appropriate tyre selection based on a number of criteria.

Here is the factor table showing the knowledge to be entered into an expert system.

Present Weather	Track Condition	Race Duration Forecast	Tyre Selection
Dry	Dry	Dry	Slicks
Dry	Dry	Rain	Slicks
Dry	Standing Water	*	Intermediates
Rain	Dry	Dry	Intermediates
Rain	Dry	Rain	Wets
Rain	Standing Water	*	Wets

Two of the rules have been written below.

IF Present Weather is Dry
AND Track Condition is Standing Water
THEN Tyre Selection is Intermediates.

IF Present Weather is Rain
AND Track Condition is Dry
AND Race Duration Forecast is Dry
THEN Tyre Selection is Intermediates.

(a) Write the rules required for Wets. **4**

(b) State which component of the expert system is used to store the facts and rules. **1**

(c) The two main methods of inferencing used in expert systems that use production rules are *backward chaining* and *forward chaining*.

(i) Describe the difference between these methods of inferencing. **2**

(ii) State which method is used in the tyre selection example. **1**

(8)

Total for Section III Part B (25)

[*END OF SECTION III—PART B—EXPERT SYSTEMS*]

SECTION III

PART C—The Internet

Attempt ALL questions in this section.

20. This diagram represents part of the network in a school.

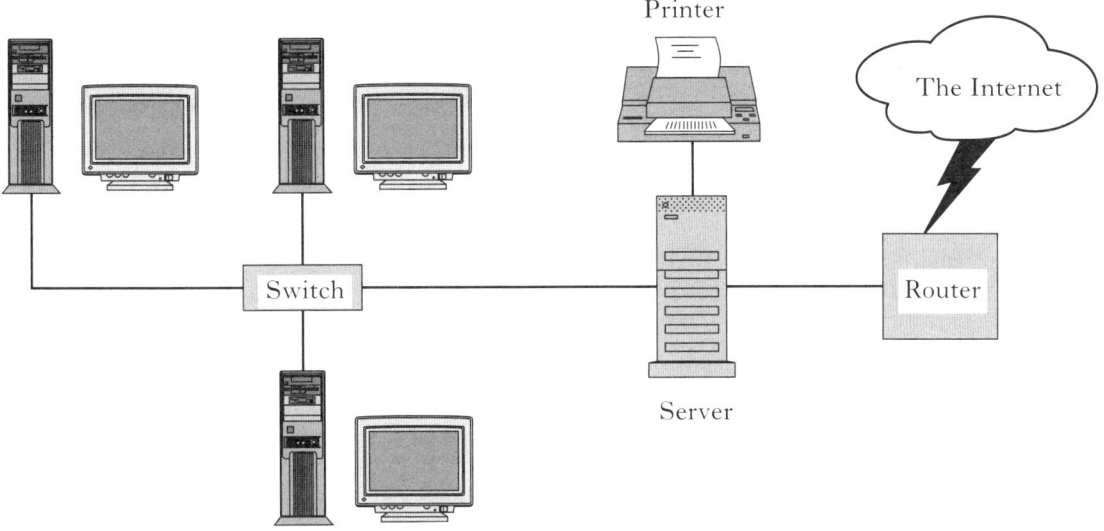

(a) (i) State the purpose of the router.

(ii) State the purpose of the switch.

(b) The school has implemented a *backup strategy*.

Why does the school need a "backup strategy"?

(c) The school's Internet connection has recently had an increase in bandwidth.

Describe **one** way pupils may notice the increase in bandwidth when using the Internet.

Marks

1

1

1

1

(4)

[Turn over

21. Sameer runs a company selling second hand books.

He has registered with an Internet Service Provider and now has access to the World Wide Web and an e-mail account.

(a) State **two** types of application software he could use to access his e-mail. 2

(b) Sameer intends to use his e-mail account to help run his business.

    (i) State **one** way he could use e-mail for business purposes. 1

    (ii) Describe how this would help in the efficiency of his business. 1

(c) Sameer wants to use a search engine to find news about auctions in Scotland, but is not interested in auctions in Edinburgh.

    (i) State a Boolean search that could be used by Sameer to find the information required. 2

    (ii) Describe **one** feature of an advanced search service that would be useful to Sameer to find the specific information he wanted. 2

(d) Sameer is using the World Wide Web and e-mail for his business.

Name **two** other Internet services that he might use. 2

(e) As Sameer travels around the country visiting book auctions, he can access the Web and his e-mail using devices other than his computer.

State **one** other device he could use to obtain Internet access. 1

(11)

Marks

22. Ally is creating a website for Holibobs, a company that sells holidays to its on-line customers.

    (a) Ally scans photographs of holiday locations from a book so they can be included on the website.

    Ally uses *picture compression*.

    (i) What is "picture compression"?   **1**

    (ii) Explain why "picture compression" is required in this situation.   **2**

    (b) Ally creates this Web page.

    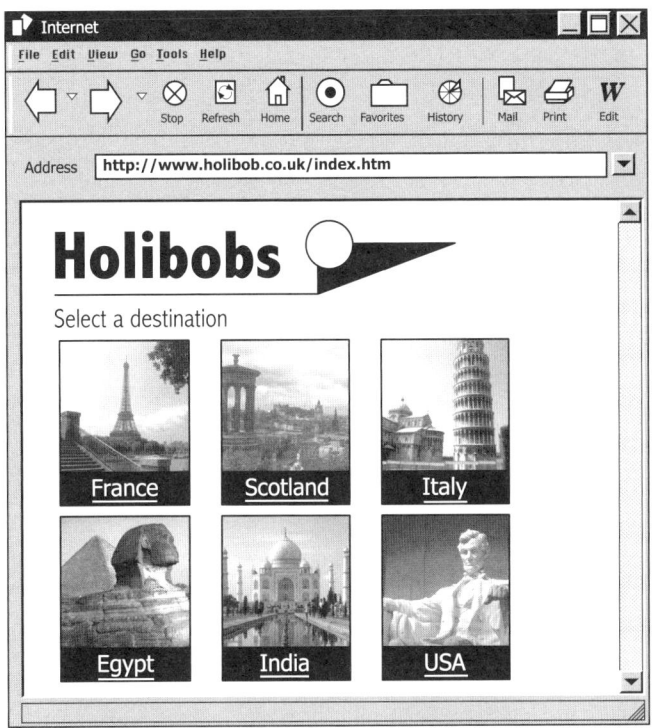

    Name the legislation Ally must comply with to include the images on the website.   **1**

    (c) Ally used Web authoring software to create the Web page. One of the features of the software was the *hyperlink tool*.

    (i) State the purpose of the "hyperlink tool".   **1**

    (ii) Describe how Ally used this tool in the Web page shown.   **1**

    (d) The address of this Web page is http://www.holibob.co.uk/index.htm. It uses the *http protocol*. Ally creates a folder in the same directory as the index page to store all the graphics for the Web page. The folder is called *images*. The graphic used for Scotland has the filename **edinburgh.jpg**.

    (i) What is a "protocol"?   **1**

    (ii) What is the purpose of the "http"?   **1**

    (iii) Using absolute addressing, write down the address of the graphic used for Scotland.   **2**

       (10)

    Total for Section III Part C   **(25)**

[*END OF SECTION III—PART C—THE INTERNET*]

[*END OF QUESTION PAPER*]

INTERMEDIATE 2
2009

X216/201

NATIONAL
QUALIFICATIONS
2009

FRIDAY, 29 MAY
9.00 AM – 10.30 AM

INFORMATION
SYSTEMS
INTERMEDIATE 2

Attempt Section I and Section II and **one** Part of Section III.

Section I – Attempt all questions.
Section II – Attempt all questions.
Section III – This section has three parts:
    Part A – Applied Multimedia
    Part B – Expert Systems
    Part C – The Internet

[Handwritten note: Only do these questions.]

Choose **one** part and answer **all** of the questions in that part.

Read each question carefully.

Write your answers in the answer book provided. **Do not** write on the question paper.

Write as neatly as possible.

Answer in sentences wherever possible.

SECTION I

Attempt all questions in this section.

Marks

1. Describe **one** difference between *data* and *information*.   1

2. The spreadsheet below shows the sales figures for a concert.

	A	B	C	D
1	Kinto Katz Ticket Sales			
2		Quantity	Price	Value
3	Front Seating	150	£11.00	£1,650.00
4	Rear Seating	150	£12.00	£1,800.00
5	Upper Seating	200	£10.00	£2,000.00
6	Standing	500	£7.50	£3,750.00
7			Total	£9,200.00

    (a) State **one** *data object* used in a spreadsheet.   1

    (b) From the spreadsheet above, identify **one** *formatting function* that has been carried out.   1

3. A travel agent allows customers to book holidays online.

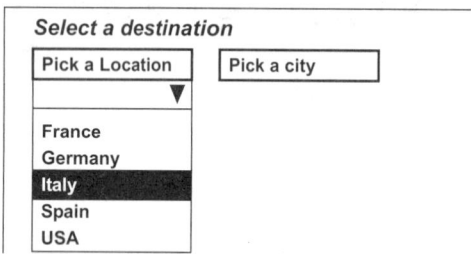

State the type of *validation* used to ensure that customers only choose holidays in countries offered by the travel agent.   1

4. Slideshows and brochures are used to advertise products.

    (a) Name the type of application software used to produce a slideshow.   1

    (b) Name the type of application software used to produce a brochure.   1

5. State **two** reasons why a company may need to have a network strategy.   2

6. State **one** advantage of using linked tables in a relational database rather than a flat file database.   1

Marks

7. The database below shows some of the results of runners taking part in the Olympic Fun Run.

No	Start	Finish	Forename	Surname	Gender (M/F)	Athletics Club
1011	10:15:00	11:12:17	Eric	Gallimore	M	www.olympicharriers.com
1475	10:15:00	11:15:33	Daniel	McHugh	M	www.olympicrunners.co.uk
2232	10:20:00	11:41:12	Vicky	Chen	F	www.ba-athleticsclub.co.uk
2246	10:20:00	11:20:04	Jembu	Malf	M	www.runforfun.org.uk

    (a) Suggest the most appropriate field type for the Start field.   1

    (b) Suggest the most appropriate field type for the Athletics Club field.   1

8. Give **one** example of how the use of technology has changed the way people shop.   1

9. The school information system shown below is used to print out a list of absentees.

ID Number	Forename	Surname	Class
20081237	Alison	Begley	1A
20081348	Anna	Smith	1A
20081872	Mirza	Hanif	1B
20081903	Patrick	McCann	1B
20082760	Charlie	McKenzie	1B
20081845	Naiem	Mohammed	1C
20082856	Eilidh	Fraser	1D
20081992	Johann	Schmidt	1D

    (a) Describe how the above list has been sorted.   2

    (b) State **one** advantage of using an electronic information system rather than a manual system.   1

Total for Section I   (15)

[END OF SECTION I]

[Turn over

SECTION II

Attempt all questions in this section.

10. PawsHome is a company with cat homes across Scotland. It stores information about its cat homes and employees on paper. A sample of the data held is shown below.

Employee Name	Gender	Age	Position	Employee No	Cat Home	City
Peter Jones	Male	34	Manager	134	HOM23	Perth
Li Chan	Female	43	Secretary	145	HOM23	Perth
Mary Smith	Female	29	Manager	234	HOM45	Inverness
Amadi Adumatta	Male	52	Secretary	265	HOM45	Inverness
Lisa Smith	Female	35	Cleaner	233	HOM19	Perth
Peter Jones	Male	36	Supervisor	237	HOM19	Perth

(a) Before the database can be implemented, the data must be normalised.

   (i) Explain why the Employee Name attribute would **not** be suitable as a primary key.   **1**

   (ii) Normalise the above table by removing the multi-valued fields, and show how it would be represented in two tables. Clearly indicate meaningful table names and the primary and foreign keys.   **7**

   (iii) State the one to many relationship between the above tables.   **1**

(b) State the type of validation check that should be used to ensure that the Age attribute cannot be left empty.   **1**

(c) PawsHome must comply with the Data Protection Act.

   (i) In terms of the Data Protection Act, state what PawsHome must do before they store personal data.   **1**

   (ii) Who is the data controller in this case?   **1**

(12)

Marks

11. John runs a car rental dealership. He has created a database and started entering data into it. The database is shown below.

Reg No	Make	Model	Engine Size (cc)	Daily Rental (£)
DCT04FT	Alpha	Siesta	1400	15
DCS04SJ	Alpha	Spring	1800	25
AEF54JY	Epsilon	Dash	1400	20
PFD53GF	Delta	Tiger	1400	20
EEE51EG	Sigma	Vector	1600	25
KTH50JJ	Alpha	Focus	1800	15

(a) A customer phones asking for a particular type of car. John used the database to output the following results.

Reg No	Make	Model	Engine Size (cc)	Daily Rental (£)
DCS04SJ	Alpha	Spring	1800	25
KTH50JJ	Alpha	Focus	1800	15

    (i) Describe how John queried the database to get the results shown above.   **3**

    (ii) What name is given to the printed output from a database?   **1**

(b) Reg No could be used as a *primary key*. What is the purpose of a "primary key"?   **1**

(c) When creating a database, John noticed that he could add an *object* type field.

State **one** type of information that would be stored in an "object" type field.   **1**

(d) Describe the purpose of the database user interface.   **1**

                                                                                                 (7)

[Turn over

12. Blush sells cosmetics in their High Street shops.

(a) Blush employs several *knowledge workers*.

Describe the job of a "knowledge worker". **1**

(b) Blush has a centralised database situated at its head office.

(i) What is meant by a centralised database? **1**

(ii) At the end of each day, Blush's information system is used to total that day's sales and to save the results on the hard disk.

State the **two** functions of this information system that are being carried out at the end of each day. **2**

(c) Angelique has just joined Blush from another cosmetics company.

(i) Angelique brought a copy of her previous employer's test results for a new lip gloss.

State **one** of the ethical implications of Blush using these test results. **1**

(ii) Before Angelique could start work, she had to sign Blush's *netiquette* agreement form.

Describe **two** rules you would expect to find on Blush's "netiquette" form. **2**

(iii) Angelique uses a computer program that contains a series of tasks that teach her how to use Blush's database software.

Name this type of program. **1**

(d) Ken is a website developer for Blush who has recently created Blush's cosmetic online shop.

(i) Name the type of software that would be most appropriate to build and maintain a complex website. **1**

(ii) With the introduction of the online shop, Blush found that their sales had increased significantly due to new customers.

Give one example of how Blush may have gained new customers through the online shop. **1**

(iii) Ken has found that a former employee has been hacking into Blush's computer system.

State the law that the former employee has broken. **1**

(11)

Total for Section II (30)

[END OF SECTION II]

SECTION III

Attempt ONE part of Section III

Part A	Applied Multimedia	Page 8	Questions 13 to 14
Part B	Expert Systems	Page 11	Questions 15 to 17
Part C	The Internet	Page 13	Questions 18 to 21

Choose **one** part and answer **all** of the questions in that part.

[Turn over

SECTION III

PART A—Applied Multimedia

Attempt ALL questions in this section.

13. A museum has decided to create interactive multimedia information points around the museum.

    (a) Below is part of the report from the analysis stage

    > ... the information points should allow visitors (targeted 8–14 year old children and their parents) to be able to see and hear the information about the exhibits without distracting other visitors around them. The refurbishment of the museum will be completed by November of this year and the information points must be created, tested and in place by then. The museum can afford to spend £15 000 on the development of the information points ...

    (i) The report on the analysis stage contains the purpose and budget available for the multimedia development. State **two** other aspects that have been considered in the above analysis report.

    (ii) Recommend the most appropriate delivery medium for the museum to use in this situation.

    (b) One of the screen designs for the presentation is shown below.

    > **EGYPTIAN PHARAOHS**
    > Shown below are the years that Pharaohs ruled. Years are BC.
    > *Sneferu ruled from 2613 to 2589,* **Khufu ruled from 2589 to 2566,** Djedefra ruled from 2566 to 2558 and Khafra ruled from 2558 to 2532.

    State **two** text design principles that have been broken in the creation of the above design.

13. (continued)

(c) One of the screens from the museum information point is shown below.

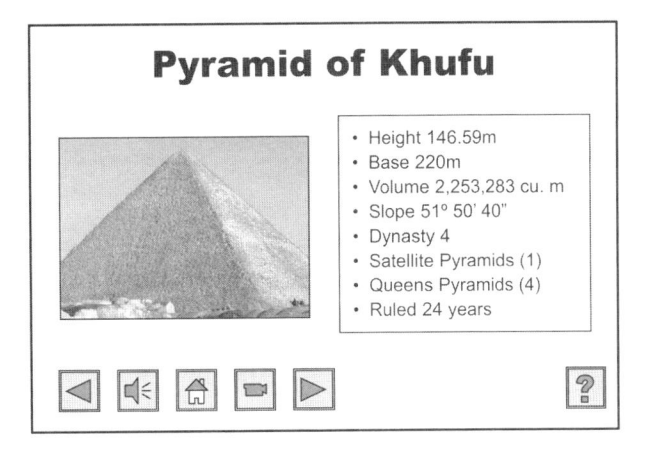

    (i) State the type of user interface being used above. **1**

    (ii) This type of interface was chosen because of its ease of use.

       State **one** reason why the interface shown above is easy to use. **1**

(d) During the testing stage, a *navigation test* was carried out.

    Explain the purpose of a "navigation test". **1**

(e) The museum evaluates the multimedia application in terms of *fitness for purpose*.

    Describe **one** method the museum could use to evaluate "fitness for purpose". **1**

(f) The completed multimedia application plays background music.

    (i) The background music was captured by sampling. Explain how the sampling rate affects the quality of the audio. **1**

    (ii) Describe **one** benefit of providing background music. **1**

(g) During the evaluation process, many museum staff complained that the background music can be repetitive and distracts them from their jobs.

    (i) Describe a **software** solution to the above problem. **1**

    (ii) Describe a **hardware** solution to the above problem. **1**

(h) If visitors to the museum are unsure how to use the multimedia application they can click on the ? button and the screen shown opposite appears.

    State the name given to this type of screen. **1**

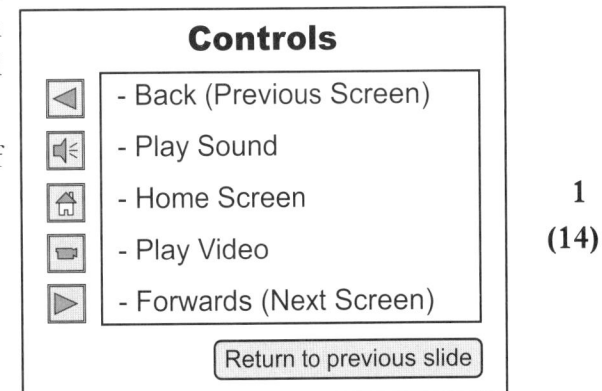

(14)

14. MultiCorp develops multimedia applications for business.

(a) State **two** examples of multimedia use for business. 2

(b) Mary is the project manager of MultiCorps's development team.

Describe **two** tasks that will be carried out by Mary as project manager. 2

(c) The design for MultiCorps's latest application is shown below.

Slide 1: Photo of flower, Camera settings (→)
Slide 2: Technical names of common flowers (← →)
Slide 3: Photo of garden, names of flowers (← →)

(i) State the type of navigation structure that would be most appropriate in this case. 1

(ii) State the type of software you would recommend MultiCorp use for this project. 1

(iii) State the job title of the person who would provide the technical knowledge that is required for the creation of slide two. 1

(d) MultiCorp's project includes 700 colour photographs which take up 6·5 gigabytes of storage. The graphic artist has been instructed to reduce the storage requirements for the photographs from 6·5 gigabytes to 3 gigabytes.

(i) Describe **two** methods of reducing the storage required for the photographs. 2

(ii) Name the storage medium that would be best suited for distributing the project to customers. 1

(iii) Some of the photographs have been copied from a website.

Which law may have been broken? 1

(11)

Total for Section III Part A (25)

[*END OF SECTION III—PART A—APPLIED MULTIMEDIA*]

SECTION III

PART B—Expert Systems

Attempt ALL questions in this section.

15. A new expert system is being developed for a travel company, to advise tourists on suitable types of holidays.

    (a) One stage of the expert system development cycle is *knowledge representation*.

    (i) State the personnel involved at the "knowledge representation" stage. **1**

    (ii) State **one** technique used at the "knowledge representation" stage. **1**

    (b) The diagram below shows a screen from the initial version of the expert system.

    > Q: Do you want a high activity holiday? [Why?]
    > **User response: yes**
    > Q: Do you want a beach location? [Why?]
    > **User response: yes**
    > Advice: You should choose a water sports holiday.
    > [Explain]

    (i) The *inference engine* is one component of an expert system.

    Identify one element shown above which was **generated** by the "inference engine". **1**

    (ii) State which component of the expert system is responsible for **displaying** "Q: Do you want a beach location?" **1**

    (iii) State which component of the expert system would be altered when a new type of holiday is added. **1**

    (iv) Describe the purpose of the "Explain" button on the screen. **1**

    (v) Describe the purpose of the "Why?" button on the screen. **1**

    (c) Describe **two** economic implications for the travel company of introducing the holiday expert system. **2**

    (d) Another expert system is being developed. This will list holiday items that should be packed. It will also provide a set of steps to follow so that tourists are organised. State the category of this expert system. **1**

    (e) Describe how querying an expert system would differ from querying a database. **2**

    (12)

Marks

16. A digital television company offers four packages to their customers, each with a different range of channels—Basic, Bronze, Silver and Gold.

The Basic package includes 15 TV channels. The Gold package allows the customer to add three more "options" to their package. The Silver package allows a choice of two out of three "options" to be added, while Bronze allows only one "option" to be added.

Shown below is **part** of the factor table showing knowledge to be entered into the expert system.

Sports Option	Movies Option	Kids Option	Package
Yes	Yes	Yes	Gold
Yes	Yes	No	Silver
Yes	No	Yes	Silver
No	Yes	Yes	Silver

(a) Complete the factor table using the knowledge available.   **4**

(b) Write a rule to represent the "Gold" package from the knowledge in the table.   **3**

(7)

17. Pat suffers from very painful joints, especially in his knees and elbows.

Pat learns about an online expert system that can be used at home to find out more about these problems.

(a) The expert system could be evaluated by its purpose and *domain* of expertise.

  (i) State the "domain" of this expert system.   **1**

  (ii) State **one other** characteristic that could be used to evaluate the expert system.   **1**

(b) Two methods of inferencing that can be used in an expert system are *forward chaining* and *backward chaining*.

  (i) Explain what is meant by "forward chaining" and "backward chaining".   **2**

  (ii) Describe **one** advantage of using forward chaining in this expert system.   **2**

(6)

Total for Section III Part B (25)

[END OF SECTION III—PART B—EXPERT SYSTEMS]

Marks

SECTION III

PART C—The Internet

Attempt ALL questions in this section.

18. Ray is configuring the latest version of an e-mail client to send and receive his e-mail. The e-mail client uses POP and SMTP protocols.

    (a) State the purpose of POP and SMTP protocols. **2**

    (b) When this message is transmitted over the Internet, it is divided into *packets*.

    Explain why the message is divided into packets. **2**

    (c) The e-mail client inserts Ray's contact details at the end of each e-mail.

    > Ray Tomlison
    > 111 Mains Water Road
    > Glasgow
    > E-mail: R.Tomlison@parpanet.org
    > Tel: 0141 496 0001
    > Fax: 0141 496 0002

    (i) State **one** reason why Ray includes contact details in the e-mail. **1**

    (ii) Describe **one** concern Ray might have about including his contact details at the end of the e-mail. **1**

    (d) Ray is concerned that a virus could be downloaded as an e-mail attachment.

    Suggest **two** methods of reducing the risk of a virus infecting Ray's computer. **2**

    (8)

19. Chumms.com is a social networking website that allows friends to keep in touch when online.

    (a) Name the Internet service that allows friends to communicate in real-time. **1**

    (b) Chumms.com allows members to share photographs. Photographs are uploaded to the member's profile page.

    Name the protocol used to upload a photo. **1**

    (c) Many schools have blocked the Chumms website to prevent pupils from accessing it.

    (i) Suggest **one** reason why schools have blocked this website. **1**

    (ii) Suggest **one** reason why pupils should be allowed access to Chumms.com. **1**

    (4)

[Turn over

20. The diagram below shows a school Web page.

(a) The layout of the Web page above has been defined using the table tool. The menu allows you to navigate from this page to other pages and the graphic animates when the pointer is moved over it.

  (i) State the feature of the Web authoring software which has been used to create the menu. **1**

  (ii) A *scripting tool* has been used to animate the graphic.

  Describe what is meant by a "scripting tool". **1**

(b) Here is the website file structure for www.school.sch.uk.

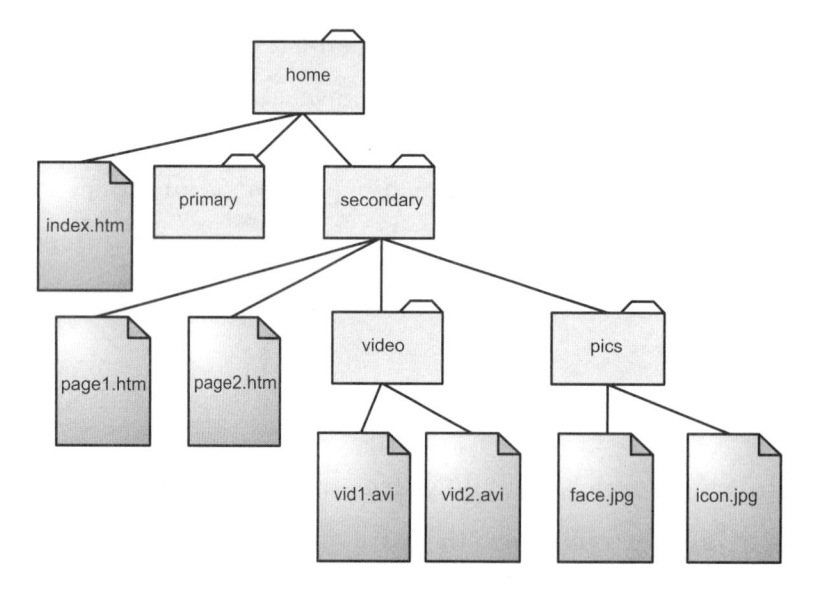

John is adding links to the **page1.htm** Web page.

  (i) State the absolute address John will enter on page1.htm to link to face.jpg. **2**

  (ii) State the relative address John will enter on page1.htm to link to icon.jpg. **1**

(c) Explain why picture compression is used on a website. **2**

(d) A browser is used to navigate from one page to another.

  Name the facility of a browser which allows you to store a Web address for later access. **1**

(8)

Marks

21. Emma's favourite band is MacFlee. She is using a search engine to find the title of MacFlee's first song.

(a) State a Boolean search that could be entered by Emma to find this information. **3**

(b) Emma wishes to listen to MacFlee's first song. Describe how Emma could use the advanced features of a search engine to find the song file. **1**

(c) When Emma selects one of the websites suggested by the search engine, several pop-up windows appear. Name the type of software you would recommend Emma installs to prevent the pop-up windows. **1**

(5)

Total for Section III Part C (25)

[END OF SECTION III—PART C—THE INTERNET]

[END OF QUESTION PAPER]

INTERMEDIATE 2
2010

[BLANK PAGE]

X216/201

NATIONAL QUALIFICATIONS 2010

THURSDAY, 20 MAY 9.00 AM – 10.30 AM

INFORMATION SYSTEMS INTERMEDIATE 2

Attempt Section I and Section II and **one** Part of Section III.

Section I – Attempt all questions.

Section II – Attempt all questions.

Section III – This section has three parts:

- Part A – Applied Multimedia
- Part B – Expert Systems
- Part C – The Internet

Choose **one** part and answer **all** of the questions in that part.

Read each question carefully.

Write your answers in the answer book provided. **Do not** write on the question paper.

Write as neatly as possible.

Answer in sentences wherever possible.

SECTION I

Attempt ALL questions in this section.

1. Define the term *data*.

2. A student uses a DVD encyclopedia to research the solar system. What type of application software is a DVD encyclopedia?

3. A mail order company uses a relational database to store information about the items it sells and who buys them. Suggest a suitable name for one of the tables in the database.

4. A field containing a numeric value can either be an *integer* or a *real* data type.

    (a) Describe what is meant by an "integer" data type.

    (b) Describe what is meant by a "real" data type.

5. Describe **one** example of how an organisation makes use of word processing software.

6. State **one** limitation of storing data in a flat file database.

7. Part of a database and part of a spreadsheet are shown below.

    Database

Record 1	
Ref No	C146
Item	Cola
Quantity	10
Price	£0·50

    Spreadsheet

	A	B	C	D
1		Product List		
2				
3	Ref No	Item	Quantity	Price
4	C146	Cola	10	£0·50
5	C123	Crisps	10	£0·50
6	J123	Juice	20	£0·40
7	S254	Mints	15	£0·25
8	S265	Chocolate	12	£0·45

    Name the data object in the spreadsheet that holds the same information as the record in the database.

Marks

8. A national organisation supplying electricity to its customers uses an information system to calculate electricity bills because it can process a large *volume* of data.

Describe **one other** reason for using an information system to calculate electricity bills.   **1**

9. Describe **one** action relating to **seating**, that an employer should implement to ensure the health and safety of employees using computers.   **1**

10. State **two** reasons for normalising data.   **2**

11. A school keeps details about pupil attendance in a database.

(a) The school prints a list of absent pupils similar to the one shown below.

Daily Absentee List		2nd September
Forename	**Surname**	**Class**
Nisah	Ali	2A
Sally	Abbot	2B
Jamie	Chalmers	2A
Jurgen	Schumacher	2A
Joyce	Watson	1D
Mo	Williams	3E

State the correct term for this printed list from a database.   **1**

[Turn over

11. (continued)

(b) During registration, a teacher enters the absentees directly into the system on the screen shown below.

	Attendance Check					
Class	2a					
Teacher	Mr Rae					
		\multicolumn{5}{c}{September}
		02–Sept	09–Sept	16–Sept	23–Sept	30–Sept
Surname	**Forename**					
Ali	Nisah	X				
Amokatchi	Nwankwo					
Ashcroft	Liam					
Barnes	Francesca					
Chalmers	Jamie	X				
Dziekanowski	Piotr					
Jones	Ciaran					
Le Pen	Thierry					
Schumacher	Jurgen	X				

State the correct term for this type of screen. **1**

12. Computers give easy access to information systems. Describe **one other** way to gain easy access to information systems. **1**

Total for Section I (15)

[END OF SECTION I]

SECTION II

Attempt ALL questions in this section.

13. XtrenIS is setting up a new information system to help run their business. XtrenIS has several branches throughout Scotland.

    (a) XtrenIS requires a new software package but are unsure which one to buy.

    The *range of data objects* available in a package is one feature that can be used to evaluate a software package.

    Name **two other** features that could be used to evaluate software packages.   2

    (b) XtrenIS has been advised to implement a *security strategy*.

    Describe **two** reasons why a company requires a security strategy.   2

    (c) XtrenIS is keen to use a *centralised database*.

    Describe **one** advantage of having a centralised database in an organisation instead of separate copies stored on different computers.   1

    (d) XtrenIS sent out the following letter to customers advising them of changes.

    ---

                                        113 Greendale Estate
                                                  Waterside
                                                    WA23 5YT

    Dear Customer

    As a valued customer, we want to keep you up to date with some of the proposed alterations to the way we run our business.

        A new information system is to be installed. This new system will involve a centralised database for customer accounts, **improved data security** and **improved customer ordering service**.

    We will be providing the same products and fine service on which we have built our reputation in the industry.

    Identify **two** formatting functions used in this letter.   2

                                                                                          (7)

[Turn over

14. Wilderness Adventures is a summer camp that employs a number of instructors to run courses for guests. Here is an example of the data stored about each instructor and the courses they run.

Instructor ID	INS186		
Firstname	Joe		
Surname	King	**Photograph**	

Course Ref	Description	Level	Day course runs
SL101	Sailing	Beginner	Monday
SL103	Sailing	Advanced	Tuesday
KY104	Canoeing	All levels	Wednesday

(a) Identify and remove the multi-value fields from the table and represent the contents as two entities with suitable names.

Clearly indicate the primary and foreign keys in the tables. **7**

(b) The personal details of each instructor are stored in the information system.

In terms of the Data Protection Act, who is the *data controller* in this situation? **1**

(c) Wilderness Adventures runs a website to advertise their courses and take bookings. The user can obtain a list of the courses available from the website.

(i) The user can only select the level of a course from a list like this:

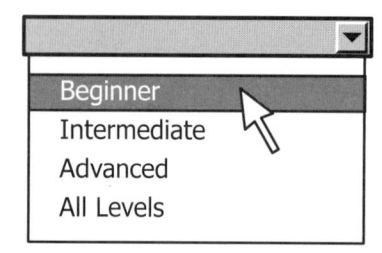

> Beginner
> Intermediate
> Advanced
> All Levels

State the type of validation used in this situation. **1**

14. (c) (continued)

(ii) Each day, Wilderness Adventures obtain a list of bookings similar to the one shown below.

Camper Number	Forename	Surname	Gender	Age	Course Ref
WA1287	Dominika	Adamczyk	Female	15	SL201
WA1007	Sally	Harkins	Female	16	KY101
WA1034	Arabella	Young	Female	14	RK101
WA1109	Jack	Greer	Male	15	AB101
WA1145	Jose	Sanchez	Male	17	SL101
WA1089	Dylan	Whitehead	Male	16	CA101
WA1345	Hussein	Zubar	Male	15	KY201

Describe how the above list has been sorted. 2

(iii) The booking list makes use of *primary keys* and *foreign keys*.

Explain what is meant by a "foreign key". 1

(d) Electronic databases can sort data into order very quickly.

Describe **two other** advantages of using an electronic database instead of a manual database. 2

(e) The user interface used on the website makes the electronic database *user friendly*.

Describe **two** other features to be considered when designing the user interface. 2

(16)

[Turn over

15. Super Lottery uses a computerised information system. Players can buy tickets for the Super Lottery from shops around the country.

(a) The functions carried out by the system are *gathering, processing, storing* and *outputting* information.

    (i) Describe **one** piece of information gathered by the system.   **1**

    (ii) Describe **one** method that could be used for entering data into the Super Lottery computer system.   **1**

    (iii) Outputting information can be done in several ways.

    Describe **one** method of output that may be used in the Lottery system.   **1**

    (iv) The computerised information system used by Super Lottery carries out a lot of processing.

    Describe **one** process that may be carried out in the Lottery system.   **1**

(b) Super Lottery is considering selling tickets online.

    (i) Describe **one** advantage to players of the Super Lottery of buying their tickets online rather than from a shop.   **1**

    (ii) Describe **two** implications for Super Lottery of selling their tickets online rather than from a shop.   **2**

    (7)

Total for Section II (30)

[END OF SECTION II]

SECTION III

Attempt ONE part of Section III.

Part A	Applied Multimedia	Page 10	Questions 16 to 18
Part B	Expert Systems	Page 14	Questions 19 to 22
Part C	The Internet	Page 18	Questions 23 to 25

Choose **one** part and answer **all** of the questions in that part.

[Turn over

SECTION III

PART A—Applied Multimedia

Attempt ALL questions in this section.

16. Argus, a high street catalogue shop, decides to replace their in-store catalogues with multimedia information screens.

    (a) Two designs for the user interface of the information screens are shown below.

    Design A

Browse Argus
1 TV & DVD
2 Kitchen Appliances
3 Photo & Camcorders
4 Gaming Software
5 Audio Products
Type the number of the option you wish:

    Design B

Browse Argus
1 TV & DVD
2 Kitchen Appliances
3 Photo & Camcorders
4 **Gaming Software**
5 Audio Products
Type the number of the option you wish:

    (i) State the type of user interface being used above. **1**

    (ii) Argus decided to use Design A. State **two** reasons, relating to text design principles, why Argus might prefer Design A. **2**

    (b) When the user moves from one screen to another, a "dissolve" effect occurs.

    (i) State the term used to describe a special effect occurring between screens. **1**

    (ii) Explain why Argus uses special effects when changing screens. **1**

    (c) Each of the 25,000 products in the multimedia catalogue requires a photograph to be stored. This has made the file size of the catalogue very large.

    It has been decided to alter the photos **without compressing them**.

    (i) Describe the method used to reduce the file size of Photo 1 to give Photo 2 that is shown below. **1**

    Photo 1   Photo 2

    (ii) Explain how the method you described in part (i) reduces the file size of the photo. **1**

16. (continued)

(d) The multimedia catalogue is updated as stock is sold so that customers know how many are left in the store.

The WWW could be used as the delivery medium. State **one other** delivery medium that could be used in this case. **1**

(e) The local newspaper is creating an online article reporting on the Argus shareholders meeting. A small part of two versions of the article are shown below.

Version 1

Argus reports record profits

"2010 has been the best year yet," reported Jim Aitchinson chairman of Argus. A smiling Jim addressed shareholders at yesterdays meeting to report record profits of £8·4 million.

Version 2

Argus reports record profits

Jim Aitchinson

"2010 has been the best year yet," reported Jim Aitchinson chairman of Argus. A smiling Jim addressed shareholders at yesterdays meeting to report record profits of £8·4 million

(i) State **two** graphic design principles that have been used when changing Version 1 into Version 2. **2**

(ii) In both versions, the photograph is an *anchor*. Describe what is meant by the term "anchor" in this situation. **1**

(11)

[Turn over

17. Blah is a digital audio player application. It allows users to store music and album art on a home computer.

(a) A typical screen contains the information on one album. The screen should contain the name of the album and the artist who recorded it, as well as a picture of the album cover and navigation buttons to move between albums.

Draw a labelled storyboard showing all of the above screen design elements. **3**

(b) When music files are captured to be stored using Blah, the user can choose from a range of *sampling rates*.

Describe what is meant by the term "sampling rate". **1**

(c) Many users of Blah download music files from the Internet without permission.

Name the piece of legislation they may have broken. **1**

(d) Blah allows users to search for music files.

State the type of search facility illustrated below.

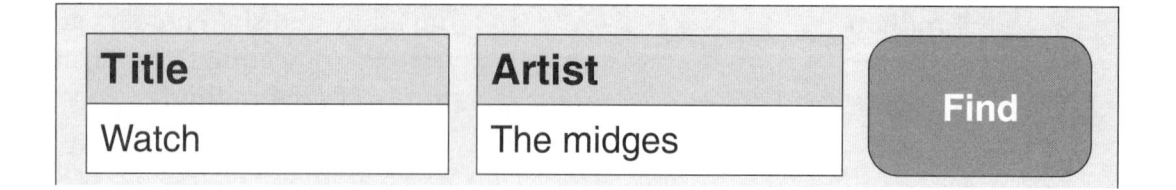

Title	Artist	Find
Watch	The midges	

1

(e) A digital audio player application is an example of multimedia used at home.

State **one** other use of multimedia at home. **1**

(f) The digital audio player application comes with *online help*.

Describe "online help". **1**

(8)

Marks

18. Netastik are creating a multimedia application to promote their business.

(*a*) When creating the multimedia application Netastik have to take account of the *audience* who will be using the application.

    (i) Describe **one** issue about the audience that Netastik should take into account when creating the application.   1

    (ii) Describe a solution to the issue you identified in part (i).   1

(*b*) State the job title of the person who organises the development of the application and ensures that it is created on time and on budget.   1

(*c*) Netastik has a choice of using an *icon-based* or *scripting* authoring package to create the multimedia application. Netastik have chosen to use the icon-based authoring package as it was easier to use.

Describe why an icon-based authoring package is easier to use than a scripting authoring package.   1

(*d*) During the testing stage, a *screen test* will be carried out. Explain the purpose of a "screen test".   1

(*e*) Netastik evaluate the mulitmedia application in terms of *fitness for purpose*.

Describe one method they could use to evaluate fitness for purpose.   1

    (6)

Total for Section III Part A   **(25)**

[*END OF SECTION III—PART A—APPLIED MULTIMEDIA*]

SECTION III

PART B—Expert Systems

Attempt ALL questions in this section.

19. Money Matters is an expert system used by university students to find out ways to earn money. The expert system asks questions to find out about the students' interests and free time. The students enter their responses and the software displays jobs they may be interested in.

    (a) Describe **two** purposes of an expert system. **2**

    (b) When the Money Matters expert system was created, an *expert system shell* was used. Describe what is meant by the term "expert system shell". **1**

    (c) State the category of expert system that Money Matters belongs to. **1**

    (d) During the consultation, the following screen is displayed:

    > Q: Is playing sport your favourite way to spend your free time?
    > A: Yes
    > Q: Is going to the cinema your favourite way to spend your free time?
    > A: No
    > Q: Is eating out your favourite way to spend your free time?
    > A: No

    Suggest a more efficient method of getting the same information. You may use a diagram in your answer if you wish. **2**

    (6)

Marks

20. Cheap and Cheerful are producing recipe sheets for university students. They wish to provide students with cheap tasty recipes. They decide to create a recipe expert system.

(a) There are three stages in creating an expert system. The first stage is knowledge acquisition. State the **other two** stages. — 2

(b) During the creation of the recipe expert system, a number of personnel will be involved. The domain expert will provide information about the recipes and foods.

   (i) State **one other** person involved in the creation of the expert system. — 1

   (ii) Describe the role of the person you identified in part (i). — 1

(c) When the expert system is complete and working, it gives the user *How* and *Why justification facilities*.

   (i) At what point during the consultation of the recipe expert system would the "Why" facility be used? — 1

   (ii) Describe the purpose of the "How" facility in the recipe expert system. — 1

(6)

[Turn over

21. TakeitEasy is a holiday company using an expert system to help customers decide where to go on holiday. Some of the rules from the expert system are shown below.

> IF price range IS expensive
> AND likely weather IS hot
> AND activities ARE scuba diving
> THEN destination IS Barbados.
>
> IF price range IS medium
> AND likely weather IS mixed
> AND activities ARE sight seeing
> THEN destination IS Prague.
>
> IF price range IS cheap
> AND likely weather IS rain
> AND activities ARE donkey riding
> THEN destination IS Blackpool.
>
> IF price range IS expensive
> AND likely weather IS snow
> AND activities ARE skiing
> THEN destination IS French Alps.
>
> IF price range IS expensive
> AND likely weather IS hot
> AND activities ARE sight seeing
> THEN destination IS Rome.

(a) When writing the rules, the creators had a choice of inferencing methods they could use.

   (i) State the type of inferencing used in the above rules.

   (ii) Explain why the creators of the expert system used this type of inferencing in this situation.

   (iii) Describe **one** feature of the *inference engine*.

(b) Mr Hamid wants a holiday which will be expensive and where the likely weather is hot and he can do some sight seeing. State the destination the expert system would recommend.

(c) Instead of using an expert system, TakeitEasy could have created a database to store this information.

   State how many fields the database would have.

(d) Compare the way TakeitEasy staff would find suitable holiday destinations using an expert system and a database.

Marks

22. The National History Museum collects information on dinosaurs.

Some of the information is represented as the following attribute-value pairs:

Guanlong (eats meat = Yes, runs fast = Yes, no of legs = 2)
Saltopus (eats meat = Yes, runs fast = Yes, no of legs = 4)
Byteosaurus (eats meat = Yes, runs fast = No, no of legs = 4)
Diploducus (eats meat = No, runs fast = No, no of legs = 4)
Graciliceratops (eats meat = No, runs fast = Yes, no of legs = 2)

Represent these attribute-value pairs as a decision tree.   5

(5)

Total for Section III Part B (25)

[*END OF SECTION III—PART B—EXPERT SYSTEMS*]

SECTION III
PART C—The Internet
Attempt ALL questions in this section.

23. Fotto.com is a website that sells photographs.

(a) The Fotto.com website has a search engine that allows the user to search for photographs on any topic. Wenling is a student who uses the Fotto.com website to find pictures.

  (i) Wenling is looking for a photograph of either a yellow or red flower, which is any type except a rose. Write down the Boolean search that would produce the required result. **3**

  (ii) Wenling copies the photograph of the flower from the website without permission. State the piece of legislation Wenling may have broken. **1**

  (iii) Wenling regularly uses the Fotto.com website. State the feature of web browser software that Wenling could use to store the location of the page for easy access. **1**

(b) All photographs on the website use *picture compression*.

  (i) Describe **one** benefit to Fotto.com of using picture compression. **1**

  (ii) Describe **one** benefit to Wenling of the Fotto.com website using picture compression. **1**

(c) Fotto.com have added a new facility that allows users of the website to upload their own photographs.

  (i) State the protocol used to upload photographs to the Fotto.com website. **1**

  (ii) A user has uploaded a photograph containing their name and address.

  Explain why having their name and address on the photograph may be inappropriate. **1**

(9)

Marks

24. The home page for BizBing.com is shown below.

(a) The home page above was created using several features of web authoring software:

- the web page has been formatted into rows and columns
- the graphic animates when the pointer rolls over it
- the menu allows you to navigate to other web pages.

(i) State the feature of the web authoring software that was used to create the rows and columns. **1**

(ii) Code was added to the website that allowed the graphic to be animated when the pointer moves over it. State the feature of web authoring software that allows code to be added to the website. **1**

(b) BizBing sell Internet security software and hardware.

(i) State **two** types of Internet security software that may be sold by BizBing. **2**

(ii) BizBing's best selling hardware device is a *router*. Describe the function of a router. **2**

(c) The BizBing website makes use of both *absolute* and *relative page addressing*. The absolute page address for the BizBing logo is:

http://www.bizbing.com/image/keylogo.jpg

(i) State what *www* stands for in the above address. **1**

(ii) Some customers instead of typing http://www.bizbing.com, enter 81.99.141.142

State what 81.99.141.142 represents. **1**

(iii) Explain what is meant by the term "absolute page addressing". **1**

(iv) Explain what is meant by the term "relative page addressing". **1**

(10)

Marks

25. Betty uses the school network for class work, accessing the Internet and video conferencing.

    (a) The school network contains a device that allows several signals to be sent down a single line at the same time. State the name of this device. **1**

    (b) Betty uses the video conferencing facility for educational purposes.

    (i) Describe **one** example of how Betty might use video conferencing for educational purposes. **1**

    (ii) When the video conferencing data is transmitted over the Internet it is divided into *packets*. Explain why the data is divided into packets. **2**

    (c) Betty's teacher has suggested that the class submit their homework answers using a newsgroup service. Explain why using a newsgroup may be unsuitable for submitting homework answers. **1**

    (d) Betty has a friend who does not have access to Internet, newspaper or library services. State the term used to describe someone who does not have access to these services. **1**

    (6)

    Total for Section III Part B **(25)**

[*END OF SECTION III—PART C—THE INTERNET*]

[*END OF QUESTION PAPER*]

INTERMEDIATE 2
2011

[BLANK PAGE]

X216/201

NATIONAL
QUALIFICATIONS
2011

MONDAY, 16 MAY
9.00 AM – 10.30 AM

INFORMATION
SYSTEMS
INTERMEDIATE 2

Attempt Section I and Section II and **one** Part of Section III.

Section I – Attempt all questions.

Section II – Attempt all questions.

Section III – This section has three parts:

      Part A – Applied Multimedia

      Part B – Expert Systems

      Part C – The Internet

Choose **one** part and answer **all** of the questions in that part.

Read each question carefully.

Write your answers in the answer book provided. **Do not** write on the question paper.

Write as neatly as possible.

Answer in sentences wherever possible.

SECTION I

Attempt ALL questions in this section.

1. Explain what is meant by the term *information system*.

2. The table below shows part of a train timetable.

Inverness (INV) to Aberdeen (ABN) Saturdays		
	\multicolumn{2}{c}{Outward Journey}	
Journey Number	1	2
Departure Station	INV	INV
Arrival Station	ABN	ABN
Departs	12:42	14:27
Arrive	14:54	16:41
Changes	0	0

   (a) Identify **one** item of *data* from the table.

   (b) Identify **one** item of *information* from the table.

3. One benefit of using an electronic database system is that *data analysis* and *reporting* can be carried out easily.

   (a) State **one** other benefit of using an electronic database system rather than a manual system.

   (b) Explain what is meant by a database *report*.

4. Here is part of a database showing the tracks on a CD.

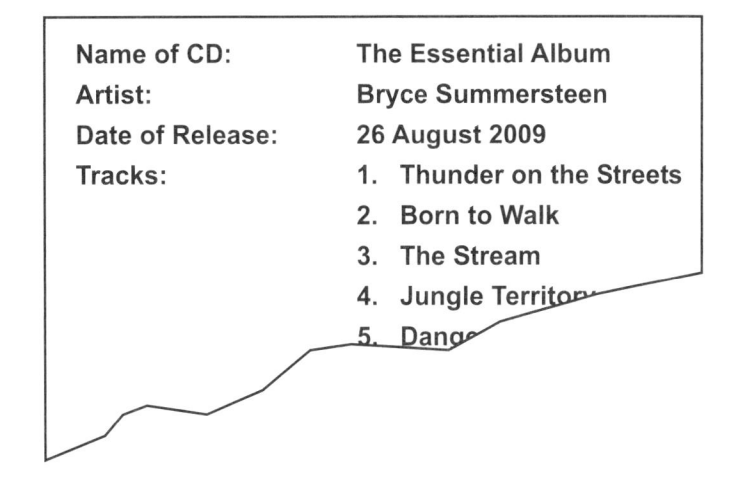

> Name of CD: The Essential Album
> Artist: Bryce Summersteen
> Date of Release: 26 August 2009
> Tracks:
> 1. Thunder on the Streets
> 2. Born to Walk
> 3. The Stream
> 4. Jungle Territory
> 5. Danger

State the relationship that exists between this CD and the tracks. **1**

5. Spreadsheet software can be used for keeping business accounts.

State **one** other suitable type of application software for keeping business accounts. **1**

6. Describe what is meant by the term *data subject* with reference to the Data Protection Act. **1**

[Turn over

7. The following table shows details of flowers for sale.

Product Code	Image	Product Name	Price (£)	Category
FL24		Sunshine	26·99	Summer
FL10		Tulip Special	37·99	Spring
FL54		Tickled Pink	28·99	Celebration
FL55		Blue Heaven	23·99	Celebration
FL59		Red Roses	39·99	Celebration
FL25		Blaze of Glory	34·99	Summer

State which Product Code would be at the top of the table when the list is sorted by Category in ascending order and by Price (£) in ascending order.

8. Explain what is meant by a *Boolean* data type.

9. The *speed, accuracy* and *volume* of data processed all determine the *efficiency* of an information system.

Explain what is meant by "speed" in relation to an information system.

10. Explain why *validation* is used in a database system.

Marks

11. The chart below shows the share of votes cast for each candidate in a class president election. In Version 1 of the chart, it was not clear who won the election so Version 2 of the chart was created.

Version 1

Votes for Class President

Version 2

Votes for Class President

23% 27%

14%

15%

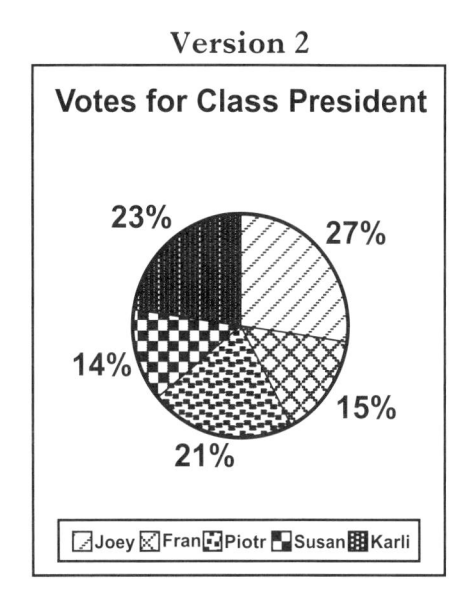

21%

Joey Fran Piotr Susan Karli

Identify **one** formatting function that has been carried out to create Version 2. **1**

12. A concert venue sells tickets from their ticket office and online from their website. State **one** benefit to shoppers of buying tickets online. **1**

13. Explain what is meant by the term *foreign key*. **1**

Total for Section I (15)

[*END OF SECTION I*]

[**Turn over for SECTION II on** *Page six*

SECTION II

Attempt ALL questions in this section.

14. Dox.com uses a range of software in different departments within their organisation.

    (a) The customer services department use a word processing application called WordExtra to write letters to customers.

    Before purchasing WordExtra, the application was evaluated in terms of *data objects*, *data operations*, the *HCI* and *online help*.

    (i) State **one** data object used in a word processing document. **1**

    (ii) Describe what is meant by "online help". **1**

    (iii) Dox.com evaluated the HCI offered by WordExtra by trying out some of the editing operations available. Part of the HCI is shown below.

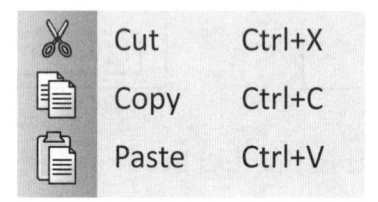

    ```
    Cut    Ctrl+X
    Copy   Ctrl+C
    Paste  Ctrl+V
    ```

    Explain, giving **two** reasons, why Dox.com liked the HCI for editing operations. **2**

    (b) Staff members send electronic messages to each other.

    State **one** type of software application that staff could use for this form of communication. **1**

    (c) The personnel department use a spreadsheet to work out if employees are entitled to a bonus.

	A	B	C	D	E	F	G	H	I
1	Forename	Surname	Monday	Tuesday	Wednesday	Thursday	Friday	Hours Worked	Bonus Due
2	Susie	Master	8	8	8	8	8	40	Yes
3	Sean	Murphy	8	7	7	8	8	38	No
4	Sasha	Ivanova	8	9	8	8	9	42	Yes
5	Samia	Anwar	8	7	7	8	9	39	No
6	Sandrine	Dupont	7	7	8	8	9	39	No

    A bonus is paid to an employee if their total number of hours worked in a week is at least 40 hours. The **calculate** and **replicate** operations are used when creating the spreadsheet.

    (i) Identify **one** cell reference from the spreadsheet above where a **calculation** has been used. **1**

    (ii) Identify a range of cells in the spreadsheet above where **replication** may have been used. **1**

14. (continued)

(d) In the sales department, the sales assistants use cash tills.

    (i) The sales assistant types the product code into the cash till when a customer buys an item.

    Describe **one** other method that could be introduced to input data about an item sold.   1

    (ii) When the product code for a sale is entered, the item name and price is displayed on the screen.

    Describe **one** other method of output that may be used in this system.   1

(e) Describe **one** area of health and safety regulations, relating to using computers at work, that Dox.com should consider.   1

    (10)

[Turn over

15. A DIY warehouse stores details about its suppliers and products.

Some of the data held is shown below.

SupplierID   C34792
Supplier Name Chark
Address   15 Mains Industrial Park
Town   Downhall
Telephone 01234567899

ProductID	Description	Price (£)	Department
AB123	Paving brush	4.98	Garden Tools
AB479	Dustpan set	5.50	Cleaning
AB604	Long handled broom	6.75	Cleaning
PT198	Wire cup brush	7.69	Power Tools
DC902	Wallpaper brush	1.55	Decorating

(a) The DIY warehouse has been advised to remove the multi-valued fields by *normalisation*.

State **two** reasons for normalising data. 2

(b) Identify and remove the multi-valued fields from the above table and represent the data as two entities with suitable names.

Identify all primary and foreign keys. 7

(c) When setting up the new database, the field called Price (£) is created using a *real* data type.

Explain what is meant by a "real" data type. 1

(10)

16. Mirkot is a mail order company that sells goods to customers. In 2009, Mirkot set up a computerised information system to handle orders.

(a) Describe **two** costs involved in setting up a computerised information system. **2**

(b) Mirkot establish a *backup strategy* to avoid losing information in the system.

State **one** reason why Mirkot need to avoid losing information. **1**

(c) After one year of using the information system, the chart below is created.

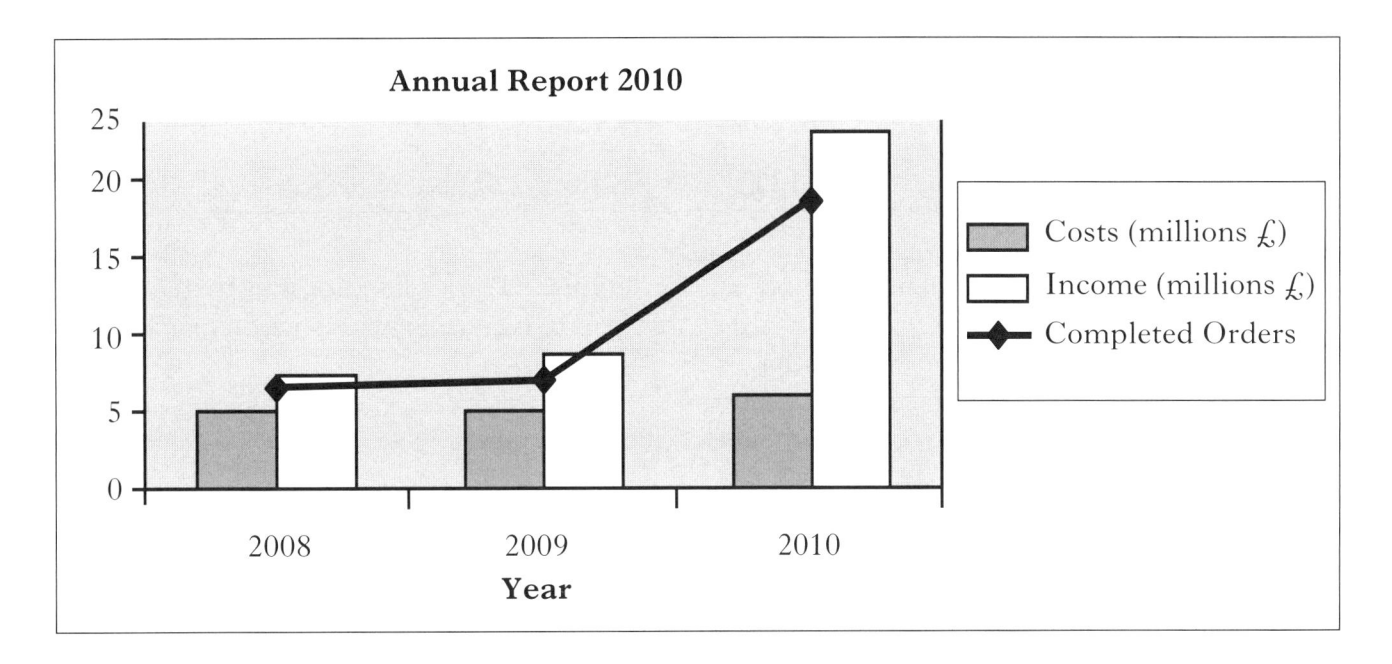

Annual Report 2010

(bar chart showing Costs (millions £), Income (millions £), and Completed Orders for years 2008, 2009, 2010)

Describe **two** economic benefits to Mirkot of introducing their computerised information system. **2**

(5)

[Turn over

17. A library uses a *flat file* database to store details about members and the books they borrow. Here is part of the file.

Membership Card ID	Member Name	Telephone	Book Reference	Book Title	Date Borrowed
KP102	Mary Smith	987265	BK234	Emma	12/3/09
KP982	James Main	967364	BK287	The Green Mile	12/3/09
KP102	Mary Smith	978265	BK290	Pride and Prejudice	02/4/09
KP982	Jimmy Main	967364	BK205	Blaze	14/4/09
KP982	James Main	967364	BK106	The Dark Tower	21/4/09
KP345	Jo Jones	911235	BK287	The Green Mile	15/5/09

A flat file database has a number of limitations. The same data is often entered several times. This duplication of data can lead to inconsistencies such as data being entered differently or incorrectly.

(a) Explain what is meant by the term "flat file database". **1**

(b) From the table above, give **one** example where data is duplicated. **1**

(c) James Main cannot remember which books he has borrowed from the library. The librarian enters the query James Main into the Member Name field.

   (i) Explain what is meant by a "query". **1**

   (ii) Explain why this query for James Main will not show all the information about books he has borrowed using his membership card. **1**

   (iii) State a query that would find all the books borrowed by James Main. **1**

   (5)

   Total for Section II (30)

[END OF SECTION II]

SECTION III

Attempt ONE part of Section III.

Part A	Applied Multimedia	Page 12	Questions 18 to 19
Part B	Expert Systems	Page 15	Questions 20 to 23
Part C	The Internet	Page 19	Questions 24 to 26

Choose **one** part and answer **all** of the questions in that part.

[Turn over

SECTION III

PART A—Applied Multimedia

Attempt ALL questions in this section.

18. Emily owns a jewellery shop.

    (a) Emily employs a company to produce a catalogue of her jewellery on CD-ROM. This catalogue will be posted out to her customers.

    (i) During the analysis stage the user must be considered.

    Describe **two** factors about the user that must be considered. 2

    (ii) Apart from the user, state **two** other aspects of the analysis stage that should be considered. 2

    (b) Michael works for the company that Emily has employed to create her CD-ROM.

    (i) Michael sketches screens to be included in the CD-ROM.

    State Michael's job title. 1

    (ii) Shown below are the first sketches made by Michael.

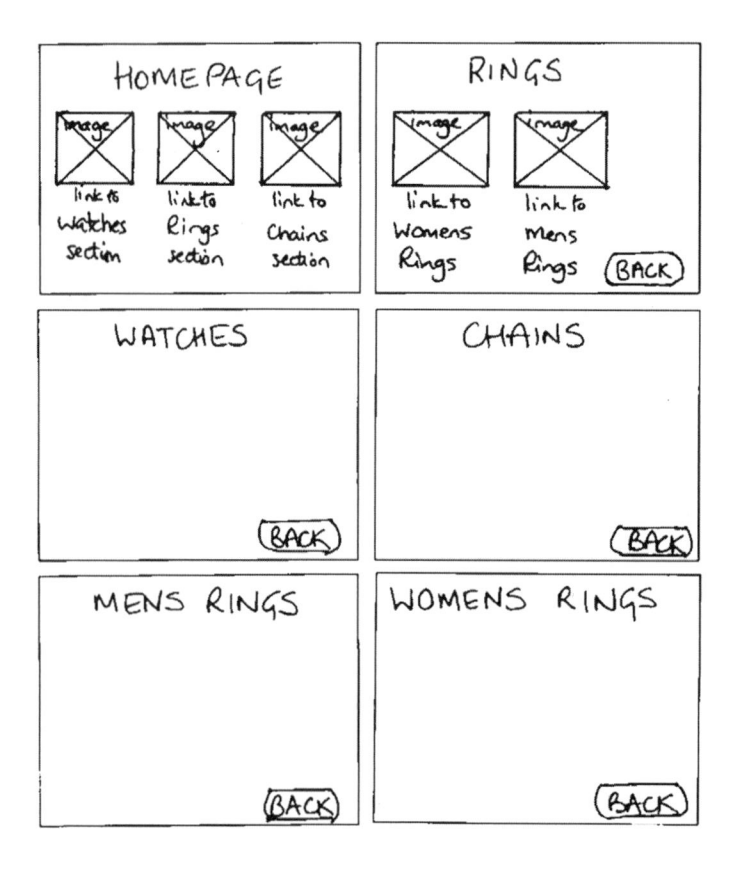

    A   Draw the navigation map structure for the sketches shown above. 2

    B   State the type of navigation structure to be used in the CD-ROM. 1

Marks

18. (continued)

(c) Michael has been asked to prepare storyboards for a new section on Earrings. He creates the storyboard shown below.

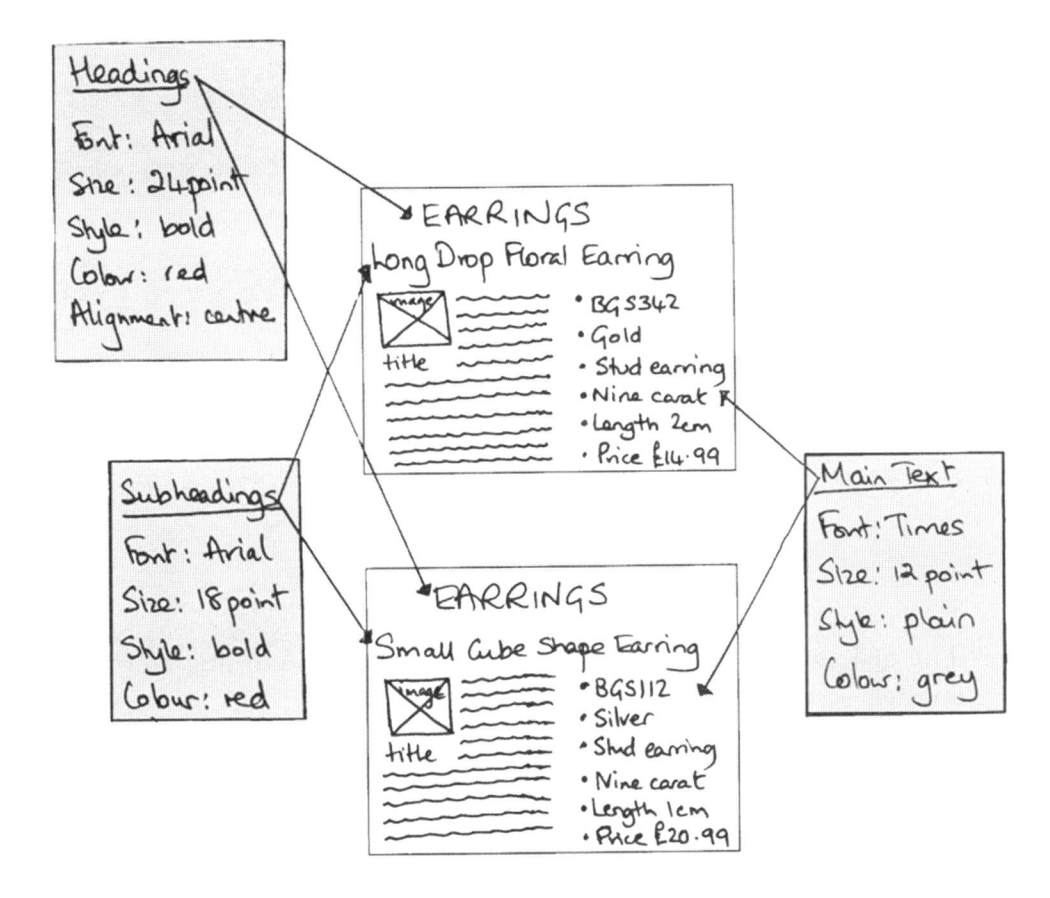

    (i) Describe **two** design principles relating to text demonstrated in the sketches above.   2

    (ii) Describe **one** design principle relating to graphics demonstrated in the sketches above.   1

(d) Some of the screens involve synchronising many complex multimedia objects.

State the most appropriate type of software for creating the CD catalogue.   1

(e) Due to the large number of high quality graphics, the catalogue requires 3·4Gb of storage. The graphics specialist has been given the job of reducing the file size.

    (i) Without altering the physical dimensions of the graphics, describe **two** methods of reducing each graphic's file size.   2

    (ii) After reducing the file size of the graphics, the catalogue still requires 1·2Gb of storage and will not fit onto a CD-ROM.

State the most appropriate delivery medium for posting the catalogue to customers.   1

                                                                                               (15)

Marks

19. GoldRiver is a shopping and leisure complex. GoldRiver plans to provide electronic public information points. These points will provide information about shop locations, catering facilities and cinema listings.

(a) (i) State the most appropriate delivery medium for the public information points.   1

(ii) State **two** reasons for your answer to part (i).   2

(b) Before the information points can be used, testing must be carried out.

(i) Explain the purpose of *screen testing*.   1

(ii) Explain the purpose of *navigation testing*.   1

(c) The information points make use of audio.

(i) State **two** possible uses of audio in GoldRiver's information points.   2

(ii) Describe how the sampling rate affects the quality of the audio.   1

(d) The information points make use of logos from different shops on some of their screens.

(i) The manager of GoldRiver is concerned about including company logos on their screens. Explain why she is concerned.   1

(ii) Describe what GoldRiver could do to ease the manager's concerns, while still including the company logos on their screens.   1

(10)

Total for Section III Part A (25)

[END OF SECTION III—PART A—APPLIED MULTIMEDIA]

SECTION III

PART B—Expert Systems

Attempt ALL questions in this section.

20. "My Little Helper" is an expert system that suggests which toys are suitable for different children.

(a) Azim provided the knowledge for the expert system.

State Azim's role in the development of the My Little Helper expert system. **1**

(b) Four screens from the expert system are shown below.

My Little Helper	My Little Helper
Who is the gift for? ○ Boy ○ Girl [Explain]	What age is the child? ○ 0–6 months ○ 6 months–1 year ○ 1 year+ [Explain]
My Little Helper	My Little Helper
What is the child interested in? ○ Cars ○ Dolls ○ Books ○ Games [Explain]	Suggested Toys: ○ Timmy Truck ○ Callum Carr ○ Connect 7 [Reason]

(i) Identify the component of the expert system shown above. **1**

(ii) Describe the main function of the component you named in part (i). **1**

(iii) From the screens above, identify the part used for *why* justification. **1**

(iv) During the development, the following information was used.

No	Input	Expected Output	Actual Output
1	Boy Age – 3 months Interest – Cars	• Timmy Truck • Bath time buddies • Trucks 'n' Cars	• Timmy Truck • Bath time buddies • Trucks 'n' Cars
2	Girl Age – 1 year+ Interest – Books	• Gerry the Giraffe by P Glancy • Everyone loves a nut by A Tree	• Connect 7 • Hungry Elephants

Identify the stage in the development process where this information would be used. **1**

(v) State **two** criteria used to evaluate an expert system. **2**

(7)

21. Darius is an expert on diamonds. Darius grades diamonds as follows.

> - If the diamond is round, clear in colour with a rough texture and no imperfections then it is graded as grade 1.
> - Square diamonds that have a smooth texture and have a few imperfections are graded as grade 2 as long as they are clear.

The first paragraph can be represented using the following attribute-value pair Grade1(shape=round, colour=clear, texture=rough, imperfections=no)

(a) Create an attribute-value pair for grade 2 diamonds. **2**

(b) Darius has been asked to work with the *knowledge engineer* to develop the expert system.

Explain the role of the "knowledge engineer". **2**

(c) Darius is considering using this expert system to grade his diamonds.

State the category of this expert system. **1**

(5)

Marks

22. PC Planet is a large computer shop. It uses an expert system to select the most appropriate computer for a customer.

(*a*) The first stage in developing PC Planet's expert system was *knowledge acquisition*. Describe what is involved in "knowledge acquisition". **1**

(*b*) State the second stage in developing the expert system. **1**

(*c*) The following advert was shown in a computer magazine.

PC Planet's Amazing Prices!!!

Basic PC
Memory – 4Gb
Hard Drive – 500Gb

Ultimate PC!!!
Memory – 8Gb
Hard Drive – 1000Gb
Internet Ready – YES!!!

In the expert system, the rule for the Basic PC is:

Computer IS Basic IF
Memory IS 4Gb AND
Hard Drive IS 500Gb.

(i) Identify the method of inferencing that has been used in the above rule. **1**

(ii) Explain your answer to part (i). **1**

(iii) Create a rule for the Ultimate PC as described in the advert above. **3**

(7)

[*Turn over*

23. "HotHair" is an expert system used by hairdressers. The information from the expert system is shown in the following decision tree.

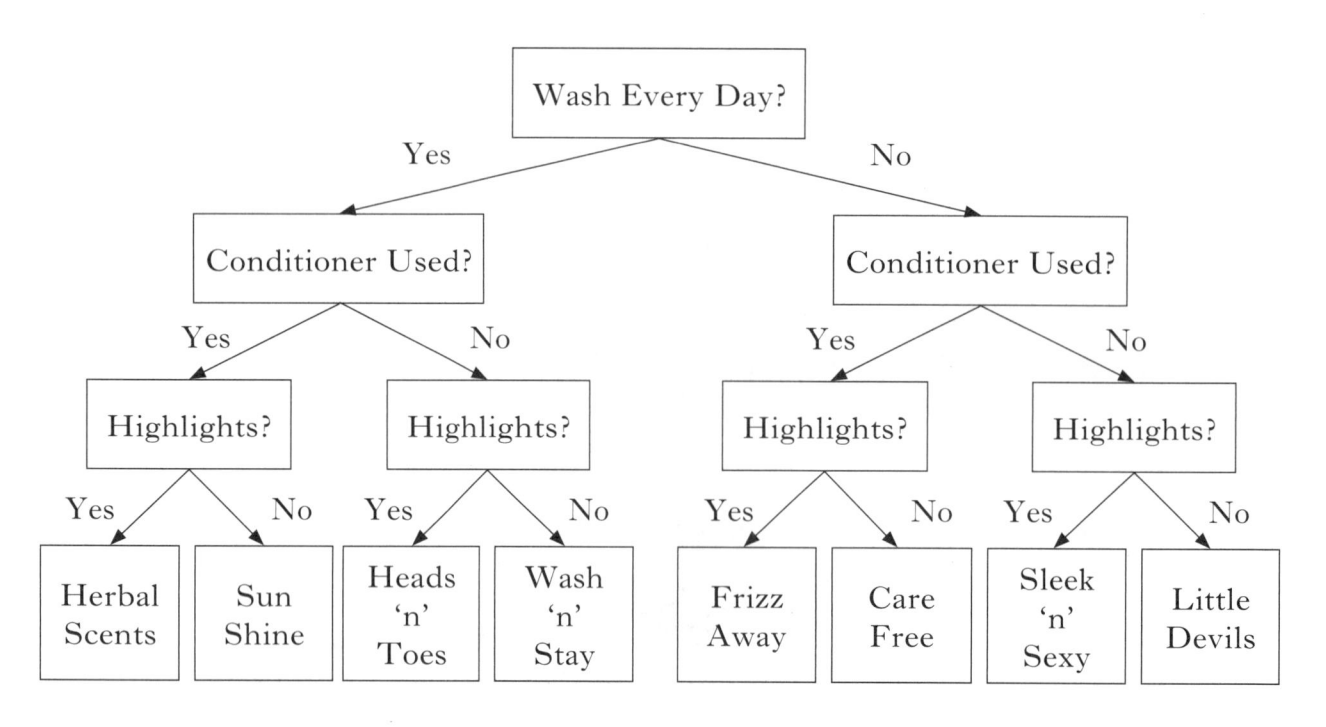

```
                        Wash Every Day?
                  Yes /              \ No
          Conditioner Used?        Conditioner Used?
         Yes /      \ No           Yes /      \ No
      Highlights?  Highlights?   Highlights?  Highlights?
      Yes / \ No   Yes / \ No    Yes / \ No   Yes / \ No
    Herbal  Sun   Heads  Wash   Frizz  Care  Sleek  Little
    Scents  Shine 'n'    'n'    Away   Free  'n'    Devils
                  Toes   Stay                Sexy
```

(a) One reason for using the HotHair expert system is to advise clients on which shampoo to buy.

Describe **two** other reasons for using HotHair. **2**

(b) Zach has highlights in his hair and needs to wash it every day but hates to use conditioner.

Identify the shampoo the HotHair expert system would recommend for Zach. **1**

(c) The HotHair expert system is going to be published on the Internet. The company are concerned about their *Information Intellectual Property Rights*.

Explain what is meant by "Information Intellectual Property Rights". **1**

(d) An alternative way to store this information is in the form of a database.

(i) How many records would the database have? **1**

(ii) How many fields would the database have? **1**

(6)

Total for Section III Part B (25)

[END OF SECTION III—PART B—EXPERT SYSTEMS]

SECTION III

PART C—The Internet

Attempt ALL questions in this section.

24. Multivalley is a new energy drinks company. The layout of their network is shown below.

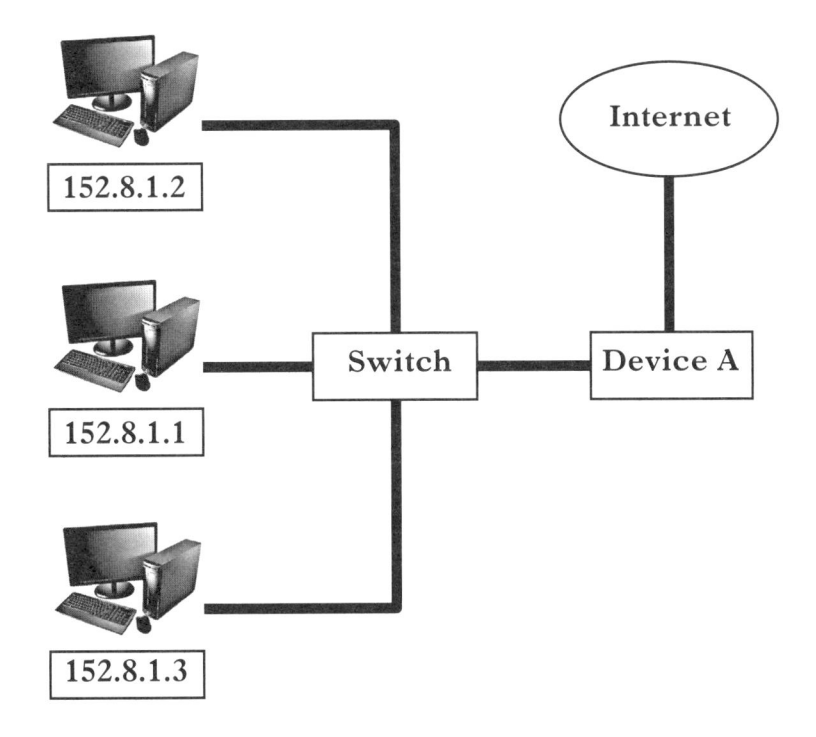

    (a) Describe the function of a *switch*. **1**

    (b) Device A is used to connect the network to the Internet.
       State the name of device A. **1**

    (c) Identify an *IP Address* from the diagram above. **1**

    (d) The *TCP/IP* protocols are used to transmit data across a network.

       (i) Describe the function of the TCP protocol. **1**

       (ii) Describe the function of the IP protocol. **1**

    (e) The directors of Multivalley are concerned about a damaging program that an employee has downloaded. The program is deleting files from the hard drives.
       Describe how Multivalley could have protected itself from this program. **2**

    (7)

[Turn over

Marks

25. Scots Ancestors Ltd is an Internet company that helps customers trace their ancestors. The company used web authoring software to create their website making use of *icon-based* features and *web tools*.

   (a) State **one** reason why "icon-based" features are easy to use. 1

   (b) The contacts page of their website is displayed using the Voyager Internet Browser.

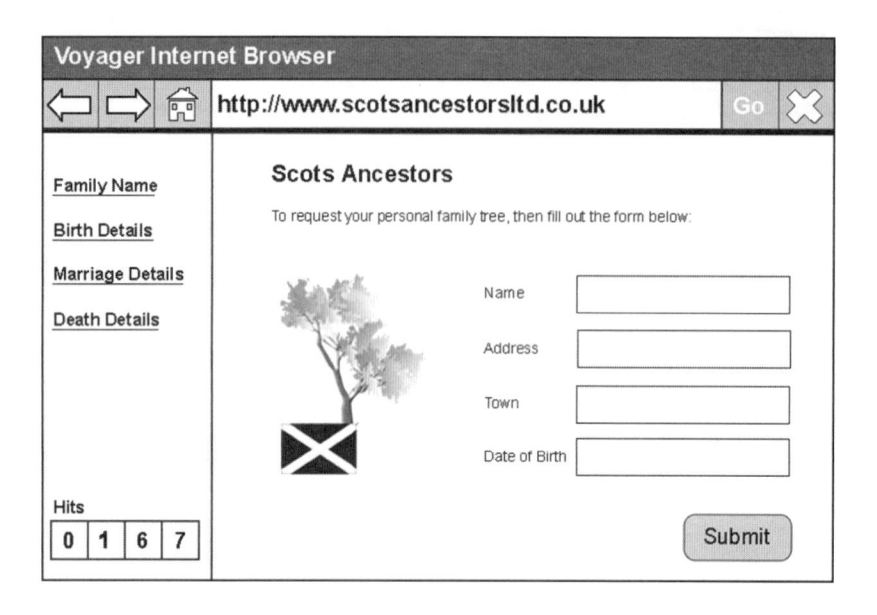

   (i) Identify **one** navigation feature present in the Voyager Internet Browser. 1

   (ii) Explain the purpose of the navigation feature you identified in part (i). 1

   (iii) The *hyperlink tool* was used in creating the Scots Ancestors Ltd contacts page.

   Identify a hyperlink in the above web page. 1

   (iv) Identify **two** features of the above web page that were created using specialist *web tools*. 2

   (c) The website contains high quality graphics. *Picture compression* has been used on the graphics.

   (i) Explain why "picture compression" is required. 2

   (ii) State a development in communications technology that has made picture compression less necessary. 1

   (d) The website design is subject to *Information Intellectual Property Rights*.

   Explain what is meant by "Information Intellectual Property Rights". 1

   (10)

[X216/201] *Page twenty*

Marks

26. Help for Africa is a charity which provides technology for use in African countries.

    (a) The charity's slogan is "Helping those who are information poor".
    Explain why many parts of Africa are classed as *information poor*. **1**

    (b) The charity is working on their latest project sending mobile phones to farmers. They create a list of farming communities in Africa that are not in mountainous regions.
    State a Boolean search that could be used to create this list. **3**

    (c) The charity publishes the following article on their website.
    "The original principle of the Internet was to allow individuals from all over the world to freely exchange information. However, we have become concerned that some governments are discussing the possibility of blocking access to certain websites. Furthermore, there is now proof that some police forces are using spyware to monitor the Internet activity of people in their country."

    (i) From the above article, identify an example of *censorship*. **1**

    (ii) From the above article, give an example of an issue that affects *privacy*. **1**

    (d) The charity communicates with their workers in Africa using e-mail. E-mail uses the SMTP and POP protocols.

    (i) State the purpose of the SMTP protocol. **1**

    (ii) State the purpose of the POP protocol. **1**

    (8)

    Total for Section III Part C (25)

[END OF SECTION III—PART C—THE INTERNET]

[END OF QUESTION PAPER]

INTERMEDIATE 2 | ANSWER SECTION

BrightRED ANSWER SECTION FOR

SQA INTERMEDIATE 2
INFORMATION SYSTEMS 2007–2011

INFORMATION SYSTEMS INTERMEDIATE 2
2007

SECTION 1

1. A table or file

2. URL, web address or hyperlink *(or example of one)*.

3. Sort Year of Registration in ascending order AND sort Mileage in descending order.

4. Presence check on Reference Number field, **or** it is a required field.

5. Spreadsheet – editing, calculation, layout (table) facilities and sorting operations

6. *Any one from:*
   - Improve workstation layout
   - Provide wrist support
   - Provide ergonomic keyboards
   - Allow short break periods
   - Vary tasks.

7. (*a*) (Original) knowledge that can be assigned protection.
   (*b*) It is stealing other peoples original ideas.

8. Computer Misuse Act

9. (*a*) Company - high cost to set up/makes more profit in the long term
   (*b*) Employee - will lose job

10. (*a*) Boolean
    (*b*) Date

SECTION 2

11. (*a*) The number of transactions handled by an Information System.
    (*b*) Someone who adds value by processing existing information to create new information
    (*c*) *Any one from:*
       - lawyer
       - teacher
       - scientist
       - doctor
       - banker

12. (*a*) (i) Web authoring
       (ii) Browser
    (*b*) (i) To combat: virus, hacking, malware *(any two)*
       (ii) Backup, software, upgrade strategies *(any two)*
    (*c*) *Any three from:*
       - easier to organise
       - update and backup information
       - easy access to up to date information
       - updated information available to the whole organisation.

13. (*a*) *Any two from:*
       - Faster search
       - faster sort
       - easier data analysis
       - easy update
       - data stored in smaller space

    (*b*) Data modelling is the process of defining the entities (relationships), fields and keys (attributes) that are required within the entities. (Or creation of data dictionary.) The result is called a data model.
    (*c*) There is only one data item in that field, or the field stores only one instance of data
    (*d*) (i) Relational
       (ii) Data has only to be entered once, because it is in a linked table

14. (*a*) (i) Instructor:
           Instructor ID, - Primary Key
           Instructor Name
           Class:
           ClassCode, - Primary key
           SportClass, Level, CostPerclass,
           InstructorID* - Foreign key
       (ii) A key is a field, or set of fields, the values of which uniquely identify a record.
    (*b*) One instructor has many classes

SECTION 3

PART A – Applied Multimedia

15. (*a*) (i) Kiosk
       (ii) *Any two from:*
          - hardwearing
          - robust
          - secure
          - touch screen
          - user-friendly
          - easy to update
          - large capacity hard drives
          - fast transfer rates for data
    (*b*) Touch screen, keyboard/mouse
    (*c*) *Any two from:*
       - purpose - clearly defined aims and objectives
       - user/audience - who will use the application once developed
       - content - what the application will contain
       - budget - how much is available to develop the application
       - timescale - what deadline, if any, has been set for the project
    (*d*) *Any two from:*
       - reduce sample resolution
       - reduce sample rate
       - compress the file

16. (*a*) Web
    (*b*) Data Protection Act
    (*c*) (i) Form fill-in *(form will be accepted)*
       (ii) *Any one from:*
          - simple data entry
          - little training needed
          - all relevant data shown

    (*d*) *Any two from:*
       - menus
       - buttons
       - hyperlinks
       - hotspots
       - search facility

(e) *Any two from:*
- table
- limited quantity of text
- appropriate use of white space
- size of font
- appropriate font
- use of bold and underline for emphasis

17. (a) Possible breach of copyright
    (b) (i) Vector
        (ii) Bitmapped
    (c) *Any two from:*
    - reduce resolution
    - reduction of colour depth
    - compress the file
    - change file format.
    (d) (i) Matching layout to design; buttons; consistency in font, size, style; visible continuity; video/audio clips run well, text spell-checked
        (ii) All links work; smooth screen transitions; no broken/out-of-date hyperlinks

PART B – Expert Systems

18. (a) *Any one from:*
    - To represent knowledge of one or more domain experts
    - To provide advice to user via a consultation
    - To provide explanations of why certain questions asked
    - To provide explanations of how conclusions reached
    (b) (i) Knowledge base contains (facts) and rules
        (ii) Determines the order in which rules are applied and questions asked (Inference Engine applies rules in order to reach a conclusion)
    (c) *Any two from:*
    - Structure/syntax/order of questions asked
    - Presentation of conclusion
    - Quality of explanation facilities
    (d) How: explains how a conclusion was reached
        Why: explains why a certain question was asked

19. (a) Classification
    (b) (i) Domain expert provides the knowledge and expertise about butterflies
        (ii) Knowledge Engineer (knowledge acquisition/elicitation) asks the domain expert questions about characteristics of butterflies in order to obtain the knowledge about butterflies and represents it in a suitable form for entry into the expert system shell (factor table, decision tree, production rules in KRL)
    (c) (i) IF   overall size IS large
        AND colour IS white
        AND other characteristic IS whitish green tinge
        THEN butterfly type IS brimstone

        IF   overall size IS large
        AND colour IS dark
        AND other characteristic IS large eyespots on wings
        THEN butterfly type IS peacock

        IF   overall size IS large
        AND colour IS dark
        AND other characteristic IS red and white bar on wings
        THEN butterfly type IS red admiral

        IF   overall size IS small
        AND colour IS blue
        AND other characteristic IS white underside
        THEN butterfly type IS common blue

        IF   overall size IS small
        AND colour IS blue
        AND other characteristic IS black veins in white fringe
        THEN butterfly type IS adonis blue
        (ii) Forward Chaining
    (d) Consult expert system to obtain solution and compare this with solution provided by domain expert.

20.

Red Light	Amber Light	Problem identified
flashing	Off	Paper Jammed
On	Off	Paper Tray Empty
Off	Flashing	Ink Cartridge Low
Off	On	Ink Cartridge Empty
On	On	Call Service Engineer

21. (a) 3
    (b) 3
    (c) 4
    (d) 3

PART C – The Internet

22. (a) 'valiant hotel' AND 'swimming pool' NOT 'London'
    (b) (i) Data Protection Act
        (ii) It uniquely identifies their booking.
    (c) FTP
    (d) The unique identification number of the host computer
    (e) (i) SMTP - sending
        (ii) POP - receiving

23. (a) PDA or Mobile phone, tablet PC
    (b) Newsgroup: you post a message and other people in the group can see it and respond at any time. No need to all be on-line at same time.
        Chat: a message is only available for the time the chat session is open. All users need to be on-line at the same time.
    (c) (i) Webcam/mic
        (ii) Company - Save money in conference expenses
             Employee - Saves time travelling

24. (a) To set links to other pages or websites
    (b) (i) Absolute page addressing requires the full pathname to be entered
        (ii) *Any two from:*
        - Pathnames are shorter
        - It is flexible – allows easy movement of pages in folders
        - Easy to update
    (c) Compress photo, crop
    (d) (i) It receives and sends data from many workstations sharing access to the Internet with one Internet connection.
        (ii) It checks IP addresses and sends packets to their correct destination.
    (e) Install Virus protection software and update it regularly.

INFORMATION SYSTEMS INTERMEDIATE 2 2008

SECTION I

1. *Any one from:*
   - Chat Client
   - Instant Messaging
   - Video Conferencing

2. Multi-valued attribute/field.

3. *Any two from:*
   - Computer Hacking
   - Distributing Viruses
   - Unauthorised modification of computer data.

4. Assistance built into the software/Assistance available through the internet.

5. Cell.

6. *Any one from:*
   - username and password
   - firewall
   - encryption

7. (a) *Any one from:*
   - letter
   - word
   - sentence
   - paragraph
   - character

   (b) *Any one from:*
   - change (font/size/style/colour/alignment)
   - cut
   - copy
   - spell-check

8. *Any two from:*
   - magnetic strip
   - bar codes
   - OCR
   - MICR
   - mark sense card

9. *Any two from:*
   - greater choice of music on-line
   - instant access to music if downloaded
   - find music more quickly by searching rather than hunting through a shop
   - saves time as able to shop from home
   - can buy individual tracks rather than entire album

10. Typing in capitals is considered to be shouting.

11. Allows different levels of users to choose their preferred method eg expert users can use shortcuts and basic users can use menus.

SECTION II

12. (a) *Any three from:*
    - easy to mis-file and thus lose a record
    - duplication of data in several records
    - searching of records is more time consuming
    - storage was bulky and took up large amount of room
    - sorting more time consuming
    - calculations have to be done manually

    (b) *Any one from:*
    - easier to find and retrieve data
    - more complex reporting can be done
    - updating of records is easier.

    (c) (i) Only one table in the database.
        (ii) *Any two from:*
        - duplication of data
        - data might not be consistent
        - inconsistent search results in multi-value fields

    (d) *Any three from:*
    - remove multi-value fields
    - to determine which tables are required
    - to determine relationships between entities
    - to allocate attributes to each entity
    - to identify primary and foreign keys.

13. (a) (i) **Pupil** (entity)
           <u>Pupil ID</u> – primary key
           <u>Pupil ID</u>, First Name, Second Name
           Instrument (entity)
           <u>Reference No.</u> – primary key
           <u>Reference No.</u>, Musical Instrument, Make, Pupil ID*
           Pupil ID* – foreign key
       (ii) One pupil can have many instruments.

    (b) Restricted choice.
    (c) Text.

14. (a) (i) Desk Top Publishing
       (ii) *Any two from:*
       - has a range of templates suitable for creating a brochure
       - has the ability to combine text and graphics
       - has advanced features like text wrap, text frames etc

    (b) Get permission from the photo copyright holder.
    (c) May contravene Data Protection Act.
    (d) (i) Web authoring software.
        (ii) *Any two from:*
        - reach a wider audience
        - easier to distribute information
        - easier to update information
        - able to use a search facility
        - able to include multimedia objects.

    (e) (i) Not having access to information sources like libraries or the Internet.
        (ii) *Any one from:*
        - no access to modern banking facilities
        - no opportunity for studies that use online facilities
        - cannot use online shopping
        - restricted employment opportunities.

SECTION III

Part A – Applied Multimedia

15. (a) *Any two from:*
    - reduced costs as no need to pay for high street shops
    - easily updated as only one copy of the data
    - reach a worldwide audience.

    (b) (i) Complex search
        (ii) Menu-driven
        (iii) *Any one from:*
        - consistent data entry
        - limits user choice to only those available
        - reduces errors as no keyboard skills required.

    (c) Form fill-in interface.
    (d) Webmaster
    (e) (i) *Any one from:*
        - to ensure users can input data reliably
        - to ensure all information can be clearly seen
        (ii) *Any one from:*
        - navigation testing
        - screen testing.
        (iii) To ensure fitness for purpose.

16. (a) (i) *Any one from:*
 - Computer Assisted Learning
 - Computer Aided Learning.

 (ii) *Any one from:*
 - help people with pronunciation of words
 - make the stories accessible to visually impaired people
 - assist people learning to read.

 (b) *Any one from:*
 - reduce sampling rate
 - reduce sampling depth (resolution)
 - compress the file

 (c) (i) *Any two from:*
 - voice output for menu choices
 - play background music
 - add sound effects to the stories.

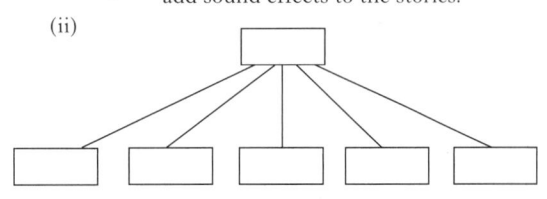

 (ii) [hierarchical tree diagram]

 (iii) Hierarchical.
 (iv) *Any one from:*
 - Scripting
 - Icon-based.

 (v) Scripting – Allows for more complex user interface to be created/allows for greater synchronisation of multimedia elements
 Icon-based – No need to learn scripting language.

 (d) A link stores the address of the destination the user will be taken to when the anchor is clicked.

 (e) (i) A transition is a visual effect as slides change.
 (ii) *Any one from:*
 - to make the change from one slide to another less abrupt
 - make the change from one slide to another more appealing

 (f) (i) Explain to the user how to use the multimedia program.
 (ii) Needed to ensure the program will work with the buyer's computer.

 (g) Copyright, Designs and Patents Act 1988.

Part B – Expert Systems

17. (a) Advice

 (b) *Any one from:*
 - Questionnaire
 - Survey
 - Interview
 - Using research materials, e.g. book, WWW, encyclopaedia.

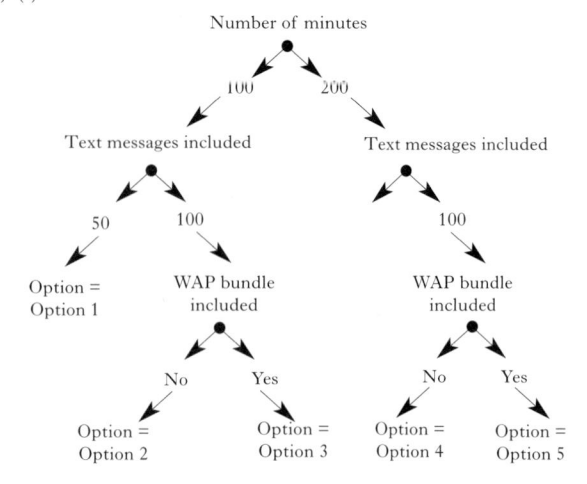

 (c) (i) [decision tree diagram: Number of minutes → 100/200 → Text messages included → 50/100, 100 → Option=Option 1, WAP bundle included → No/Yes → Option=Option 2, Option=Option 3, Option=Option 4, Option=Option 5]

 You could start with Text Messages, Minutes or WAP bundle. All are acceptable.
 (ii) Knowledge engineer.

18. (a) (i) How and Why.
 (ii) How – the customer is able to get the reasons why a certain phone has been recommended
 Why – the customer is able to get an explanation of why certain questions were asked.

 (b) Database – output is a report.
 Expert system – output is advice.

 (c) Compare results obtained from the expert system with answers from domain expert.

19. (a) IF   Present Weather is Rain
 AND   Track Condition is Dry
 AND   Race Duration Forecast is Rain
 THEN Tyre Selection is Wets.

 IF   Present Weather is Rain
 AND   Track Condition is Standing Water
 THEN Tyre Selection is Wets.

 (b) Knowledge base.

 (c) (i) Backward chaining – starts with a hypothesis and gathers evidence to prove that hypothesis.
 Forward chaining – starts by asking questions and draws a conclusion from the responses.
 (ii) Forward chaining.

Part C – the Internet

20. (a) (i) Router is used to forward packets to the correct destination by checking its IP address.
 (ii) Switch is used to forward data to another device in a local area network.

 (b) To ensure that pupil data is not accidentally lost and can be recovered if necessary.

 (c) *Any one from:*
 - Web pages displayed faster in browser
 - files download faster

21. (a) Browser/E-mail client
 (b) (i) Communicate with customers
 (ii) E-mail is faster than normal post so orders can be received and dispatched more quickly.

 (c) (i) Auctions AND Scotland NOT Edinburgh
 (ii) *Any one from:*
 - Restrict language of web sites found (to English) – would stop Sameer receiving websites that he would not be able to understand.
 - Restrict file types – If Sameer was looking for a particular file type then it would restrict the results to that one file type.
 - Using weighted keywords – would allow Sameer to have the most useful results ranked higher.

 (d) *Any two from:*
 - file transfer
 - conferencing
 - newsgroups
 - chat

 (e) *Any one from:*
 - PDA
 - Mobile phone

22. (a) (i) A method used to reduce the file size of a picture.
 (ii) Scanned images have a very large file size so compression required so that the web page will download faster for customers

 (b) Copyright, Designs and Patents Act.

(c) (i) Used to create links between web pages.
　　(ii) Hyperlink tool was used to create links from the index page to each country's page.
(d) (i) An agreement or standard set of rules.
　　(ii) For data transfer on the World Wide Web.
　　(iii) http://www.holibob.co.uk/images/edinburgh.jpg

INFORMATION SYSTEMS INTERMEDIATE 2 2009

SECTION I

1. *Any one from:*
   - Data is raw/unprocessed facts and figures (whereas information is processed data.)
   - (Data has no context whereas) information is data in context so it has meaning.

2. (a) *Any one from:*
   - Cell
   - Row
   - Column
   - Sheet
   - Range
   - Chart

   (b) *Any one from:*
   - Left align column A
   - Centre align column B
   - Right align column C or D
   - Change cell attributes to currency C1..D7
   - Change size, style font of cell A1
   - Merge cells A1..D1
   - Change column width of column A

3. Restricted choice

4. (a) Presentation

   (b) Publishing (word processing/desktop publishing/DTP/Desk Top Publisher)

5.
   - To plan how to set up the network
   - To manage its distribution of data effectively

6. *Any one from:*
   - No data duplication
   - No data inconsistency
   - No data insertion anomalies
   - No data deletion anomalies

7. (a) Time

   (b) Link (hyperlink)

8. *Any one from:*
   - Self checkout at supermarket
   - Ordering groceries online/using Internet
   - Look up items in stock using terminals in shop
   - Use of chip and PIN at checkout
   - Self serve/payment pumps at petrol stations

9. (a) Class ascending order AND Surname ascending order

   (b) *Any one from:*
   - Increased speed
   - Increased accuracy
   - Ability to process large volumes of data quickly
   - Increased efficiency
   - Searching can be performed much more quickly
   - Sorting can be performed much more quickly
   - Calculating can be performed much more quickly
   - Improved methods of data retrieval make information more easily available to users
   - Data integrity is improved, resulting in more accurate information
   - Takes up less storage space
   - Easier to update

SECTION II

10. (a) (i) *Any one from:*
- Two people could have the same name.
- There are two employees called Peter Jones.
- May need to change in future.

(ii) Cat Home(<u>Cat Home</u>, City)
Employee(<u>EmployeeNo.</u>, Employee Name, Gender, Age, Position, Cat Home*)

(iii) One cat home has many employees.

(b) Presence (check)

(c) (i) *Any one from:*
- Notify the Information Commissioner
- Register with the Data Protection Registrar
- Get data subjects' permission

(ii) PawsHome

11. (a) (i) • Search (1 mark) Make field for Alpha (1 mark) AND Engine Size field = 1800 (1 mark)

or

- Search (1 mark) Make field for Alpha (1 mark) AND Model field for Spring OR Focus (1 mark)

or

- Any other search that would give the correct table from the database shown.

(ii) Report

(b) To uniquely identify a record/row

(c) *Any one from:*
- Picture/image/graphic
- Sound/audio
- Video/animation

(d) • To allow the software and user to interact with each other.
- To make databases easier to use.

12. (a) Someone who processes or analyses information.

(b) (i) *Any one from:*
- One copy of a database that services (can be accessed by) the whole organisation.
- Single database that stores all of an organisation's data

(ii) • Processing information
- Storing information

(c) (i) *Any one from:*
- Would infringe the other employer's Information Intellectual Property Rights
- Gives company an unfair advantage
- Breach of trust

(ii) • Don't use language that would be offensive to others.
- Don't use all capital letters in e-mails.

(iii) Online tutorial

(d) (i) Web Authoring Software

(ii) *Any one from:*
- People in other countries would be able to buy their goods who could not get to their shops.
- Disabled people who could not get out of the house could shop online.

(iii) Computer Misuse Act

SECTION III

Part A – Applied Multimedia

13. (a) (i) *Any two from:*
- User/audience
- Timescale
- Content

(ii) Kiosk

(b) • Restrict number of fonts
- Use of lists and tables/bullet points

(c) (i) Direct Manipulation/GUI

(ii) *Any one from:*
- Uses standard icons/symbols to signify actions
- No requirement for keyboard skills
- Don't need to remember commands

(d) *Any one from:*
- Check all links work
- Check no broken or out-of-date links

(e) *Any one from:*
- Comparing application to the original specification
- Focus group
- User questionnaire
- User observation

(f) (i) The higher the sampling rate the better the audio quality.
(ii) May enhance the information by adding atmosphere.

(g) (i) Provide user-controlled volume controls.
(ii) Provide headphones.

(h) Online help/User documentation

14. (a) *Any two from:*
- Advertising and selling products
- Presentations
- Training
- Simulation

(b) *Any two from:*
- Coordinates the team members/ensures team are doing their job correctly
- Deals with customers to ensure they are happy with the design and final project
- Controls budget
- Controls timescales
- Allocates tasks to rest of team

(c) (i) Linear
(ii) Presentation
(iii) Subject expert

(d) (i) *Any two from:*
- Reduction of resolution
- Reduction of colour depth
- Compress the file **or** save it as a JPEG

(ii) DVD-ROM/DVD-R/DVD-RW
(iii) Copyright, Designs and Patents Act

Part B – Expert Systems

15. (a) (i) Knowledge engineer.

(ii) *Any one from:*
- Decision trees
- Factor tables

(b) (i) *Any one from:*
- 'Do you want a high activity holiday?'
- 'Do you want a beach location?'
- 'Advice: You should choose a water sports holiday'.

(ii) User interface
(iii) Knowledge base
(iv) Explains how the advice/conclusion was reached.
(v) Explains why the question is being asked.

(c) *Any one from:*
- Reduce time taken to find suitable holidays for customers (1 mark) will lead to better customer satisfaction (1 mark)

or

- Holiday company will incur large development cost of expert system (1 mark) but may recoup cost through improved profitability (1 mark)

or
- Holiday company may incur large development cost of expert system (1 mark) but could reduce wages/bills as less need for staff (1 mark).

(d) Planning

(e)
- Database: set up search query criteria or set up SQL query
- Expert system: respond to structured questions asked in an interactive manner

16. (a)

Sports Option	Movies Option	Kids Option	Package
Yes	No	No	Bronze
No	Yes	No	Bronze
No	No	Yes	Bronze
No	No	No	Basic

(b) IF 'Sports option' IS Yes
AND 'Movies option' IS Yes
AND 'Kids option' IS Yes
THEN Package IS Gold.
or
ADVISE Package IS gold
IF 'Sports option' IS Yes
AND 'Movies option' IS Yes
AND 'Kids option' IS Yes.

17. (a) (i) Illnesses/medical conditions
  (ii) *Any one from:*
   - Range and coverage of rules
   - Quality of user interface (structure/syntax/order of questions asked, presentation of conclusion, quality of explanation facilities)

 (b) (i)
   - Forward chaining is when you know the initial facts working to a conclusion.
   - Backward chaining is starting with the conclusion and working to find the facts to justify that conclusion.
  (ii)
   - Starts from known facts such as painful joints (1 mark), to reach diagnosis more directly rather than guessing hypothesis and finding facts to support it (1 mark).
   or
   - With so many possible hypotheses (1 mark), too many symptoms to eliminate if backward chaining used (1 mark).

Part C – The Internet

18. (a)
 - POP – protocol used to receive mail from the server
 - SMTP – protocol used to send/transmit e-mail across the network

 (b)
 - Allows message to be transmitted over several routes: to increase network efficiency. **or**
 - So that if the message is intercepted only that block can be read and not the whole message. **or**
 - So if message is corrupted then only that packet needs to be resent not whole message. **or**
 - Multiple users can use the network without waiting for other users to complete data transfer.

 (c) (i) In case someone wants to contact him using phone, fax or postal mail.
  (ii) His details may be used to send spam e-mails or junk mail.

 (d) *Any two from:*
 - Use virus-scanning software to detect and remove viruses
 - Update anti-virus software regularly
 - Delete or ignore messages with attachments from people he does not know

19. (a) Chat **or** Instant messaging/Conferencing/Video Conferencing

 (b) FTP **or** File Transfer Protocol.

 (c) (i) *Any one from:*
  - Prevent pupils/students wasting time
  - Inappropriate content
  - Keeping pupils safe
  (ii) *Any one from:*
  - Allows pupils/students to communicate with other pupils/students/friends.
  - Censorship is inappropriate in this situation.
  - Encourages collaborative working.
  - Reduces Nanny State culture.

20. (a) (i)
  - Hyperlink tool
  - Text tool
  (ii) A tool that allows programs/code to be written.

 (b) (i) http://www.school.sch.uk/secondary/pics/face.jpg
  (ii) pics/icon.jpg

 (c) *Any two from:*
 - to reduce the file size
 - so that it does not require a lot of bandwidth
 - to allow the page/photo to load more quickly

 (d) Bookmark **or** Favourites.

21. (a)
 - MacFlee
 - AND First
 - AND Song
 or
 - MacFlee
 - AND "First Song"

 (b) *Any one from:*
 - Select an audio search
 - Add filetype mp3 or wav or wma

 (c) *Any one from:*
 - Anti-Spyware
 - Anti-Malware
 - Pop-Up Blocker

INFORMATION SYSTEMS INTERMEDIATE 2 2010

SECTION I

1. *Any one from:*
- Data is raw/unprocessed facts and figures
- Data has not been put in context to give it any meaning
- Data is what is entered/stored in an information system

2. • Reference

3. • Any suitable table name such as PRODUCT, CUSTOMER, ORDER

4. (a) • Integer is a number with no decimal/fractional part
(b) • Real is a number which may have decimal/fractional part

5. Any suitable example for an **organisation**.
- Type letters to customers/suppliers etc (must be applied to an organisational use)
- Type memo/report/newsletter

6. *Any one from:*
- Data duplication
- Data inconsistency or update/deletion/insertion anomalies
- Data integrity errors (due to data inconsistency)
- Inconsistent search results in multi-value fields

7. Row

8. *Any one from:*
- Speed of processing – very fast
- Accuracy of calculations – no errors, very precise
- Efficiency improved

9. *Any one from:*
- Provide adjustable height chairs
- Provide swivel chairs
- Provide chairs with adjustable back
- Provide footrests

10. *Any two from:*
- To remove multi-valued fields/remove repeating group
- To establish the entities
- To establish which attributes belong in each entity
- To establish relationships between entities
- To avoid update/deletion/insertion anomalies
- To overcome the limitations of flat files (including prevent data duplication/data inconsistency errors)
- Identify both primary and foreign keys

11. (a) • Report
(b) • Data input form

12. *Any one from:*
- Mobile phone with internet access
- Computer games console connected to internet
- Interactive TV and services
- Library / mp3 player/ Sat nav/ Digital TV / Kiosk / Internet

SECTION II

13. (a) *Any two from:*
- Range of data operations/functionality
- Formatting function
- HCI (User Interface)
- Online help
- Online tutorial

(b) • To ensure that the company's important operational data is not lost or damaged by computer failure or viruses
• To ensure data is not accessed by unauthorised employees (hackers) or competitors

(c) *Any one from:*
- Easier to organise, edit, update (less data duplication, better data integrity)
- Easier to back-up the data
- Improved productivity and efficiency of business

(d) *Any two from:*
- Change style (to bold and italic)
- Right alignment of address
- Change line length of paragraph 2

14. (a) • INSTRUCTOR(instructor_ID , firstname, surname, photograph)
• COURSE(course_ref, description, level, day course runs, instructor_ID*)

(b) *Any one from:*
- Wilderness Adventures
- Summer Camp

(c) (i) • Restricted Choice
(ii) • Field called 'Gender' into ascending order
 • AND field called 'surname' into ascending order
(iii) • Foreign key is an attribute which appears in another table as a primary key

(d) *Any two from:*
- Searching can be done very quickly / more easily
- Data can be updated very quickly / more easily
- Data analysis and reporting can be done very easily
- Searches and sorts are done accurately
- Easier to backup
- Less space taken up
- Less likely to lose a record

(e) *Any two from:*
- Layout on each screen/screen design
- Method of interaction
- Choice of font/size/styles
- Consistency of layout
- Accessible to all users

15. (a) (i) • Players choice of numbers
(ii) *Any one from:*
- Scan
- OMR/Mark Sense
- Type at keypad
- Voice recognition
- Barcode

(iii) *Any one from:*
- Printed ticket issued to player
- Selected numbers sent to file for inclusion in the draw
- Selected numbers or charge displayed on screen at POS

(iv) *Any one from:*
- Search stored tickets to find numbers matching winning numbers
- Sort numbers selected into ascending order
- Count total number of tickets sold
- Calculate total prize fund
- Count total number of winners
- Pick winning numbers

(b) (i) *Any one from:*
- Can buy at time convenient to them
- No need to travel to shop
- Easy to repeat same numbers many times
- Winnings paid directly into account
- No worries about losing ticket

(ii) *Any two from:*
- Very large initial cost to establish online operation
- Must ensure secure system for purchasing

- May need to review staffing in shops if more business online
- Potential of wider audience may lead to improved profitability

SECTION III
Part A – Applied Multimedia

16. (a) (i) • Menu
    (ii) • Consistent (left) alignment of text
        • Consistent use of size of text
    (b) (i) • Transition
        (ii) *Any one from:*
            • Gives the user a visual cue that the screen is changing
            • Makes the presentation more interesting
    (c) (i) • Reduce the picture resolution
        (ii) • Fewer dots per inch need to be stored, therefore reducing the file size
    (d) • Kiosk
    (e) (i) • Text wrap
        • Caption
        (ii) *Any one from:*
            • The part of a hyperlink that you click upon
            • Either end (source or destination) of a link

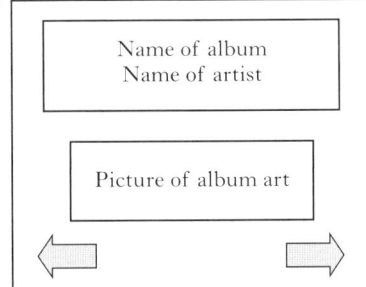

17. (a) [Diagram: Name of album / Name of artist box above Picture of album art box, with left and right arrows below]

    (b) • The number of sound samples taken per second
    (c) • Copyright, Designs and Patents Act
    (d) • Complex Search
    (e) • Computer games or any other example/category
    (f) • A built-in guide to assist the user with a feature of the software (answer needs indication of both online and help)

18. (a) (i) *Any one from:*
        • May require different languages for world wide market
        • Reading age
        • ICT capability
    (ii) *Any one from:*
        • Language translation required
        • Use of language appropriate to the targeted reading age audience
        • Easy to use User Interface
    (b) • Project manager
    (c) *Any one from:*
        • No need to learn a programming language/scripting commands
        • User simply needs to drag icons onto a timeline
    (d) *Any one from:*
        • Implementation matches design
        • Various media are displayed/played correctly
        • Hotspots are placed correctly
    (e) *Any one from:*
        • Compare application to original specification
        • Focus Group
        • User Questionnaire
        • User Observation

Part B – Expert Systems

19. (a) *Any two from:*
    • To represent the knowledge of one or more human experts
    • To provide explanations of why questions are being asked
    • To provide explanations of how conclusions were reached
    • To provide advice
    • To classify
    • To plan
    • To diagnose
    (b) • With an Expert system shell the user interface and inference engine already exist – Money Matters only need supply the facts and rules.
    (c) • Advice
    (d) *A variety of answers would be acceptable*
        Only one question should be asked
        Only one response required which allows all 3 answers as shown in the question
        E.g.
        How do you spend your free time?

        | Playing sport |
        | Going to the cinema |
        | Eating out |

20. (a) • Knowledge representation
        • System validation / System testing
    (b) (i) *Any one from:*
        • Knowledge engineer
        • Programmer
        • User
    (ii) *Any one from:*
        • Knowledge engineer – works with the domain expert, writes down the knowledge so that it can be entered into the knowledge base
        • Programmer – enters the facts and rules into the expert system
        • User – client – the person or company who has commissioned the expert system
        • User – end user – the person who eventually uses the completed expert system
    (c) (i) • Why facility is used when a question is being asked
        (ii) • The how facility explains to the user how the conclusion was reached

21. (a) (i) • Forward Chaining
        (ii) *Any one from:*
            • Finds out their holiday requirements and draws a conclusion in an efficient manner
            • That is the way it would be done in a travel agency, ask the customer what they wish and make a suggestion based on their requirements
        (iii) *Any one from:*
            • To determine the order in which rules are applied
            • To determine the order in which questions are asked
            • To arrive at the conclusion
    (b) • Rome
    (c) • 4
    (d) • Using a database the staff would search the table by entering the criteria in the correct fields. When they run the search the appropriate destinations are shown as a list
        • Using an expert system the expert system displays questions that the staff answer (with responses from the clients) and an appropriate destination is given as a conclusion

22.

```
              Eats meat
           yes        no
            ↓          ↓
        Runs fast   Runs fast
        yes  no    yes   no
         ↓    ↓     ↓     ↓
       No. of No. of No. of No. of
       legs  legs  legs  legs
        ↙ ↘    ↓    ↓     ↓
        2  4   4    2     4
        ↓  ↓   ↓    ↓     ↓
   Guanlong Saltopus Byteo-  Gracili-  Diplodocus
                    saurus  ceratops
```

Part C – The Internet

23. (a) (i) *Any one from:*
- Flower AND (Red OR Yellow) NOT Rose
- Red Flower OR Yellow Flower NOT Rose

(ii) • Copyright, Designs & Patents Act

(iii) *Any one from:*
- Favourites
- Bookmark

(b) (i) *Any one from:*
- Will reduce the file size of a photograph
- So more photos can be stored on their hard disc

(ii) *Any one from:*
- Photos can be downloaded in a shorter time
- Photos can be downloaded over dial-up connection

(c) (i) • FTP

(ii) • Any reason relating to privacy or safety
- They may receive unsolicited (electronic) mail
- Strangers might recognise him in public

24. (a) (i) • Table tool

(ii) • Scripting tool

(b) (i) *Any two from:*
- Anti-Virus;
- Anti-Spyware;
- Anti-Malware;
- Pop-up blocker;
- Firewall;
- Anti-Phishing
- Encryption
- Filtering

(ii) • It checks IP addresses
- and sends the packets to their correct destination

(c) (i) • World Wide Web

(ii) • IP address

(iii) • This is when the full pathname is used to address a resource

(iv) • A relative page address gives the path to the resource relative to its current location

25. (a) • Multiplexer

(b) (i) *Any one from:*
- To communicate with a teacher or tutor
- To chat with people in other countries about her studies
- To chat with other students about her studies

(ii) *Any one from:*
- Allows message to be transmitted over several routes; to maintain network efficiency
- No need to resend entire message if 1 packet lost/corrupted.

(c) • Newsgroups are not private so homework could be copied by other students

(d) • Information Poor

INFORMATION SYSTEMS INTERMEDIATE 2 2011

SECTION I

1. *Any one from:*
- A system used by individuals or organisations to manage information
- A system that carries out processing of data

2. (a) *Any one from:*
- INV
- ABN
- 12:42

(b) *Any one from:*
- departure station – Inverness
- arrives – 16:41
- changes – 0

3. (a) *Any one from:*
- Searching can be done very quickly
- Sorting can be done very quickly
- Data can be updated very quickly
- Searches and sorts are done accurately
- Takes up less space
- Easier to backup
- Automatic calculations (calculated fields)
- Can be shared on a network

(b) • Printed results (output) from a database
- **Formatted** results of a query

4. • 1 CD has many tracks

5. *Any one from:*
- Financial
- Database

6. • A person who has their personal data stored by an organisation

7. • FL55

8. • An attribute that can only store one of two values e.g. true/false

9. *Any one from:*
- Rate of processing items
- Rate of data entry to system

10. *Any one from:*
- To ensure that data entered into a field is sensible
- To ensure that data conforms to certain restrictions/guidelines
- To reduce errors when entering data

11. *Any one from:*
- Change pattern of segment
- Add chart legend
- Display percentage values of each segment
- Pie chart has been scaled

12. *Any one from:*
- Buy tickets at anytime
- Can buy tickets for distant locations without need to travel there

13. • A primary key from another table

SECTION II

14. (a) (i) *Any one from:*
- Character
- Word
- Line
- Sentence
- Paragraph
- Page
- Image/graphic
- Table

(ii) • On screen instructions to provide assistance.
(iii) *Any two from:*
• keyboard commands available
• menu options available
• icons available
• different types of interaction available
• software is suitable for different abilities of workers

(b) *Any one from:*
• E-mail (client)
• Chat (client)
• Browser
• Instant messaging

(c) (i) • H2, H3, H4, H5, H6, I2, I3, I4, I5, I6
(ii) • (C1..G1) **or**
• (H2..H6) **or**
• (I2..I6) **or**
• (F2..F6) **or**
• (C2..G2) **or**
• Other acceptable range of cells from the diagram

(d) (i) • By scanning the bar code
(ii) *Any one from:*
• Printed receipt
• Output to file

(e) *Any one from:*
• Seating should be height and back adjustable
• Lighting should be reflected to reduce glare
• Precautions should be taken to prevent Repetitive Strain Injury (RSI)
• Regular eye tests and breaks from using the computer should be given to reduce the possibility of eye strain
• Lead aprons should be provided to employees concerned about radiation

15. (a) *Any two from:*
• Identify which attributes belong in each table
• Identify the tables that are required
• Identify the relationships between the tables
• Remove data duplication
• Remove data inconsistency
• Remove anomalies
• Remove insertion anomaly
• Remove deletion anomaly
• Remove modification anomaly
• Remove multi-valued fields
• Identify primary **and** foreign keys

(b) SUPPLIER(supplierID, supplier name, address, town, telephone number)
PRODUCT(productID, description, price, department, supplierID*)

(c) • Item of data that is a number which has a decimal/fractional part

16. (a) *Any two from:*
• Initial costs – hardware, software, installation of system (networking/hardware, etc)
• Training staff to use new system
• Employing new **specialist** staff

(b) *Any one from:*
• Mirkot cannot continue to run without data to work with – cannot access files for customers/products/suppliers/etc
• Customer loss of confidence in Mirkot if they cannot function so take business to another company

(c) *Any two from:*
• Increased productivity (increased number of orders)
• Increased profitability (increased revenue/income)

17. (a) • All data held in one table
(b) *Any one from:*
• BK287
• The Green Mile
• KP102
• Mary Smith
• KP982
• 967364

(c) (i) • Processes (searching and/or sorting) carried out to extract information from a file
(ii) *Any one from:*
• Jimmy Main and James Main are the same person
• Only finds James Main's loans, not Jimmy Main's yet they have the same membership card ID
(iii) *Any one from:*
• Query Membership Card ID field for KP982.
• Query Member name = James Main OR Member name = Jimmy Main

SECTION III

Part A – Applied Multimedia

18. (a) (i) *Any two from:*
• Age group
• Computer expertise
• Accessibility
• Geographical location (Language Spoken)
(ii) *Any two from:*
• Purpose of the CD
• Content of the CD
• Budget
• Timescale for completion

(b) (i) • Multimedia designer
(ii) (A)

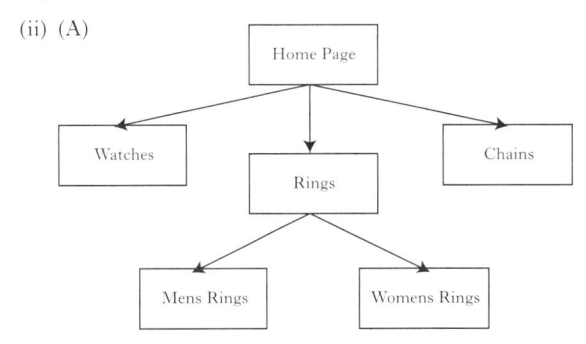

```
                    Home Page
                  /     |     \
            Watches   Rings   Chains
                     /     \
               Mens Rings  Womens Rings
```

(B) • Hierarchical

(c) (i) *Any two from:*
• Consistency in headings/body text
• Use of lists/bullet points for main points
(ii) *Any one from:*
• Use of text wrap
• Use of caption on graphic
• Consistent alignment/positioning of graphics

(d) *Any one from:*
• Authoring
• Scripting
• Icon based

(e) (i) *Any two from:*
• Reduce the colour depth
• Reduce the resolution
• Compress the graphic
(ii) • DVD-ROM

19. (a) (i) • Kiosk
   (ii) *Any two from:*
   • Has a large capacity to hold lots of information
   • Has a fast data transfer rate
   • Touch screen is user friendly
   • Robust
   • Easy to update

(b) (i) *Any one from:*
   • Make sure the text is spell checked
   • Ensure layout is correct (matches design)
   • Ensure graphics are not pixelated
   • Make sure the audio clips run well
   (ii) *Any one from:*
   • Ensures hyperlinks work correctly
   • Ensures there are smooth transitions between screens

(c) (i) *Any two from:*
   • Voice output for menu choices/narration
   • Playing background music
   • Playing sound clips from films shown in the cinema
   (ii) *Any one from:*
   The higher the sampling rate the better the sound quality

(d) (i) • Logos may be copyright (idea of copyright is essential)
   (ii) Get permission from the copyright holder to use the logos

Part B – Expert Systems

20. (a) • Domain Expert

(b) (i) • User interface
   (ii) *Any one from:*
   • To ask questions and get answers from the user
   • To display advice
   • To display the justification for asking particular questions
   • To display the justification of the conclusion reached by the expert system
   (iii) • Explain button
   (iv) *Any one from:*
   • Testing
   • System Validation
   (v) *Any two from:*
   • The purpose (ie type of Expert System and domain)
   • Range or coverage of rules
   • Quality of the user interface
   • Structure of questions
   • Presentation of conclusion
   • Quality of explanations

21. (a) • Grade2(shape=square, colour=clear, texture=smooth, imperfections=yes)

(b) *Any two from:*
   • Obtaining the domain knowledge from the expert (Darius)
   • Representing this information using a suitable Knowledge Representation Language (KRL)
   • Testing the system operated correctly

(c) • Classification

22. (a) • Gathering the knowledge required for the expert system

(b) • Knowledge representation

(c) (i) • Backward Chaining
   (ii) • Starts with hypothesis and looks for supporting evidence
   (iii) Computer   IS   Ultimate   IF
         Memory   IS   8Gb   AND
         Hard Drive ␣S   1000Gb   AND
         Internet Ready IS Yes.

23. (a) • To represent the knowledge of many hairdressers
   • To provide explanations as to choice of shampoo

(b) • Heads 'n' Toes

(c) *Any one from:*
   • Original knowledge which can be assigned legal protection
   • Legal property rights over creations of the mind, both artistic and commercial

(d) (i) • 8
   (ii) • 4

Part C – The Internet

24. (a) • To direct messages to a particular computer

(b) • Router

(c) *Any one from:*
   • 152.8.1.1
   • 152.8.1.2
   • 152.8.1.3

(d) (i) • TCP divides/combines the message into packets
   (ii) • IP provides the (source and destination) addresses and routes packets around the network

(e) *Any two from:*
   • Install virus protection software
   • Update virus protection software regularly
   • Install filtering software
   • Exclude certain file types eg .exe
   • Install firewall

25. (a) *Any one from:*
   • Picture gives an indication of the tools function
   • No need to learn commands

(b) (i) *Any one from:*
   • Back Button
   • Forward Button
   • Home Button
   • Address Bar
   (ii) *Any one from:*
   • Back Button – goes to the last page visited
   • Forward Button – retrace steps to pages visited since you last pressed back button
   • Home Button – returns to the page marked as your home page
   • Address Bar – goes to an exact web address
   (iii) *Any one from:*
   • Family Name
   • Birth Details
   • Marriage Details
   • Death Details
   (iv) *Any two from:*
   • The submit button
   • The hit counter
   • The navigation bar
   • The form fill-in fields

(c) (i) *Any two from:*
   • To reduce the file size of the image
   • So that it downloads quickly
   (ii) *Any one from:*
   • Broadband
   • ADSL
   • Cable
   • Fibre Optic - allows transmission at higher bandwidths
   • Faster Router
   • Faster download speeds

(d) *Any one from:*
- Original knowledge which can be assigned legal protection
- Legal property rights over creations of the mind, both artistic and commercial

26. (a) • They do not have access to information such as newspapers, books and the WWW

(b) • Africa
- AND farming communities
- NOT mountainous regions

(c) (i) • Blocking access to certain websites
   (ii) • Using spyware to monitor the Internet activity of people in their country

(d) (i) • Sending e-mail
   (ii) • Receiving e-mail

Hey! I've done it

© 2011 SQA/Bright Red Publishing Ltd, All Rights Reserved
Published by Bright Red Publishing Ltd, 6 Stafford Street, Edinburgh, EH3 7AU
Tel: 0131 220 5804, Fax: 0131 220 6710, enquiries: sales@brightredpublishing.co.uk,
www.brightredpublishing.co.uk

Official SQA answers to 978-1-84948-201-1
2007-2011